FREEMASONRY
MANKIND'S
HIDDEN ENEMY

"For since generally no one is accustomed to obey crafty and clever men so submissively as those whose soul is weakened and broken down by the domination of the passions, there have been in the sect of the Freemasons some who have plainly determined and proposed that, artfully and of set purpose, the multitude should be satiated with a boundless license of vice, as, when this had been done, it would easily come under their power and authority for any acts of daring."
—Pope Leo XIII
Humanum Genus
Paragraph 20

D1527994

FREEMASONRY

MANKIND'S
HIDDEN ENEMY

With Current Official Catholic Statements

SECOND EDITION
Expanded

Bro. Charles Madden, O.F.M. Conv.

> *"Let no man think that he may for any reason whatsoever join the Masonic sect, if he values his Catholic name and his eternal salvation . . ."*
> —Pope Leo XIII
> (*Humanum Genus*)

TAN BOOKS AND PUBLISHERS, INC.
Rockford, Illinois 61105

TAN BOOKS AND PUBLISHERS, INC.
P.O. Box 424
Rockford, Illinois 61105
2005

"The Freemasons follow this principle above all: 'Catholicism can be overcome not by logical argument but by corrupted morals.' And so they overwhelm the souls of men with the kind of literature and arts that will most easily destroy a sense of chaste morals, and they foster sordid lifestyles in all phases of human life. . . ."

—St. Maximilian Kolbe
(See page 34)

Table of Contents

Introduction

This book is a compilation of several articles which appeared in the *Mission of the Immaculata* in 1990 and 1991 and is an answer to numerous requests over the years from members of the Knights of the Immaculata for information on Freemasonry. St. Maximilian Kolbe especially singled out the conversion of the Freemasons as one of the main purposes in founding the Knights of the Immaculata in 1917 (See Appendix A).

This book is not intended to be an exhaustive examination of all facets of Freemasonry, but rather a basic explanation of this non-Christian religion. Due to unfortunate confusion arising in recent years, Catholics have been joining Freemasonry under the mistaken impression that the movement is no longer anti-Christian, is no longer proscribed and is nothing more than a humanitarian association. A reading of this book will show that none of these beliefs is true.

An official Catholic pronouncement from Rome and an in-depth report prepared for the U.S. Bishops are included in the Appendices.

—Bro. Charles Madden, O.F.M. Conv., 1995

FREEMASONRY

MANKIND'S
HIDDEN ENEMY

"What refers to domestic life in the teaching of the Naturalists is almost all contained in the following declarations: That marriage belongs to the genus of commercial contracts, which can rightly be revoked by the will of those who made them, and that the civil rulers of the State have power over the matrimonial bond; that in the education of youth nothing is to be taught in the matter of religion as of certain and fixed opinion; and each one must be left at liberty to follow, when he comes of age, whatever he may prefer. To these things the Freemasons fully assent; and not only assent, but have long endeavored to make them into a law and institution. For in many countries, and those nominally Catholic, it is enacted that no marriages shall be considered lawful except those contracted by the civil rite; in other places the law permits divorce; and in others every effort is used to make it lawful as soon as may be. Thus the time is quickly coming when marriages will be turned into [nothing more than] another kind of contract—that is, into changeable and uncertain unions which fancy may join together, and which the same when changed may disunite."

—Pope Leo XIII
Humanum Genus
Paragraph 21

Chapter 1

Mankind's Hidden Enemy

From time to time the National Center of the *Militia Immaculata* receives letters from members and others asking various questions about Freemasonry. People especially want to know why St. Maximilian Kolbe singled out for opposition this ostensibly fraternal organization above other anti-Christian movements such as Socialism and its various branches: Fascism, Nazism and Communism.

We intend to answer many of these questions in this book, using the sources listed in the footnotes.

A. Why Freemasonry is the "Hidden Enemy"

In the U.S.A., Freemasonry has a benign reputation among most people, including many Catholics. Hence we refer to it as the "Hidden Enemy"—*hidden* because Freemasonry is a secret society; *enemy* because both by word and deed it has proved itself again and again implacably hostile to *all* Christianity, and in particular to the Catholic Church. It has shown itself a corrupting influence on all mankind.

1. Freemasonry's secret, unceasing struggle against religion

In his encyclical letter on Freemasonry, *Humanum Genus* (1884), Pope Leo XIII equated it with the kingdom of Satan, using St. Augustine's image of the two cities, the City of man and the City of God, and the everlasting struggle between the two.

> At every period of time each has been in conflict with the other, with a variety and multiplicity of weapons and of warfare, although not always with equal ardor and assault. At this period, however, the partisans of evil seem to be combining together and to be struggling with united vehemence, led on or assisted by that strongly organized and widespread association called the Freemasons. No longer making any secret of their purposes, they are now boldly rising up against God Himself. They are planning the destruction of holy Church publicly and openly, and this with the set purpose of utterly despoiling the nations of Christendom, if it were possible, of the blessings obtained for us through Jesus Christ our Saviour.[1]

2. Freemasonry's teachings, aims and actions

After reviewing what he and his predecessors had done over the previous 150 years to combat this evil, Pope Leo XIII explored the teachings, aims and actions of this movement, pointing out that even if the several bodies which make up Freemasonry no longer remain completely concealed,

> they are still found to retain the nature and the habits of secret societies. There are many things like mysteries which it is the fixed rule to hide with extreme care, not only from strangers, but from very many members also; such as their secret and final designs . . .[2]

> Candidates are generally commanded to promise—nay, with a special oath, to swear—that they will never, to any person, at any time or in any way, make known the mem-

---

1. *Humanum Genus,* encyclical letter of Pope Leo XIII on Freemasonry, 1884, no. 2.
2. Ibid., no. 9.

bers, the passes or the subjects discussed. Thus, with a fraudulent external appearance and with a style of simulation which is always the same, the Freemasons, like the Manichees of old, strive, as far as possible, to conceal themselves and to admit no witnesses but their own members.[3]

They also promise total obedience to their leaders and a willingness to undergo severe penalties, including death, should they disobey.[4] Despite concerted efforts to lie and conceal their aims,

> . . . that which is their ultimate purpose forces itself into view—namely, the utter overthrow of that whole religious and political order of the world which the Christian teaching has produced, and the substitution of a new state of things in accordance with their ideas, of which the foundations and laws shall be drawn from mere "Naturalism."[5]

3. How Naturalism molds all Masonic beliefs and endeavors

Naturalism makes human nature and human reason supreme in all things and denies that anything has been revealed by God or that there is any teaching authority established by God. The Freemasons' constant endeavor is

> that the office and authority of the Church may become of no account in the civil State; and for this same reason they declare to the people and contend that Church and State ought to be altogether disunited. By this means they reject from the laws and from the commonwealth the wholesome influence of the Catholic religion; and they consequently imagine that States ought to be constituted without any regard for the laws and precepts of the Church.[6]

---

3. Ibid.
4. Ibid.
5. Ibid., no. 10.
6. Ibid., no. 13.

They also seek to hinder the work of the Church in every way possible and to destroy the papacy itself. Freemasonry not only attacks the Catholic religion but undermines all religion:

> . . . Again, as all who offer themselves are received, whatever may be their form of religion, they thereby teach the great error of this age—that a regard for religion should be held as an indifferent matter, and that all religions are alike. This manner of reasoning is calculated to bring about the ruin of all forms of religion.[7]

This is aimed especially at Catholicism, the only true religion. It leads to a weakening in the belief in the very existence of God. Consequently, one after another, other truths fall, so that the teaching of morality to youth, which Freemasons say they favor, is devoid of all religious foundation and belief. Even the consequences of Original Sin are denied, thus placing an exaggerated confidence in natural virtue.

4. How Freemasonry corrupts all human society

This in turn leads to a general decline in the moral standards of society that some Freemasons seek to exploit:

> For since generally no one is accustomed to obey crafty and clever men so submissively as those whose soul is weakened and broken down by the domination of the passions, there have been in the sect of the Freemasons some who have plainly determined and proposed that, artfully and of set purpose, the multitude should be satiated with a boundless license of vice, as, when this has been done, it would easily come under their power and authority for any acts of daring.[8]

---

7. Ibid., no. 16.
8. Ibid., no. 20.

Laws are favored concerning marriage and education which would secularize these two aspects of life entirely and put them completely into the hands of the State. Political doctrines are advocated which hold

> that no one has the right to command another; that it is an act of violence to require men to obey any authority other than that which is obtained from themselves.[9]

5. The links between Freemasonry, ancient pagan religions, Socialism and Communism

Pope Leo XIII goes on to say that the Freemasons desire to reinstate the manners and customs of ancient pagan religions. Furthermore, he states that Freemasons favor the designs of Socialists and Communists to overthrow established governments everywhere. Moreover, they seek to deceive both rulers and their peoples by pretending friendship on the one hand, and by flattery on the other, all the while urging the people to assail both the Church and the civil power.[10]

B. The Church's basic, unchanging response to Freemasonry

1. Exposure

Pointing out that there can be no compromise with Freemasonry, Pope Leo XIII told the world's Bishops:

> We pray and beseech you, Venerable Brethren, to join your efforts with Ours, and earnestly to strive for the extirpation of this foul plague . . . We wish it to be your rule first of all to tear away the mask from Freemasonry, and to let it be seen as it really is.[11]

---

9. Ibid., no. 22.
10. Ibid., nos. 24, 27, 28.
11. Ibid., no. 31.

> Let no man think that he may for any reason whatsoever join the Masonic sect, if he values his Catholic name and his eternal salvation as he ought to value them. Let no one be deceived by a pretense of honesty. It may seem to some that Freemasons demand nothing that is openly contrary to religion and morality; but, as the whole principle and object of the sect lies in what is vicious and criminal, to join with these men or in any way to help them cannot be lawful.[12]

2. Positive countermeasures

The Pope then proposed a variety of means to counteract this evil: widespread religious instruction with clergy and laity working together; vigorous promotion of the Third Order of St. Francis so as to have a wholesome strengthening effect on society; establishing or reviving solid, religion-based guilds for the protection of workmen and to get men away from evil associations; the promotion of the St. Vincent de Paul Society and its work among the poor; and finally, steadfastness in prayer, invoking the intercession of Our Lady, St. Michael, St. Joseph and the Apostles Peter and Paul.

3. Fact: Freemasonry continues unchanged today

Today, over a century after Leo XIII issued *Humanum Genus*, the Church's fundamental statement on Freemasonry, some in the Church assume that what this great Pope wrote about Freemasonry is either no longer true or is at least now greatly mitigated. Such is not the case! The Freemasons are still a secret society; they still continue to conceal their mysteries and designs, even from their own members. In one of their official fundamental source books, *Morals and Dogma*, we find the following:

> Masonry, like all the Religions, all the Mysteries, Hermeticism and Alchemy, *conceals* its secrets from all except the

---

12. Ibid.

Adepts and Sages, or the Elect, and uses false explanations and misinterpretations of its symbols to mislead those who deserve only to be misled; to conceal the Truth, which it calls Light, from them, and to draw them away from it. Truth is not for those who are unworthy or unable to receive it, or would pervert it. So God Himself incapacitates many men, by color blindness, to distinguish colors, and leads the masses away from the highest Truth, giving them the power to attain only so much of it as it is profitable to them to know. Every age has a religion suited to its capacity.[13]

Secrecy is indispensable in a Mason of whatever Degree. It is the first and almost the only lesson taught to the Entered Apprentice.[14]

The Blue Degrees [most Masons never go beyond these— Author] are but the outer court or portico of the Temple. Part of the symbols are displayed there to the Initiate, but he is intentionally misled by false interpretations. It is not intended that he shall understand them; but it is intended that he shall imagine he understands them. Their true explication is reserved for the Adepts, the Princes of Masonry . . . It is well enough for the mass of those called Masons, to imagine that all is contained in the Blue Degrees.[15]

In more than one way, deception is practiced on those entering into the First Degree of Masonry, that of the Entered Apprentice. After being assured that nothing in the oath he is about to take will conflict with his religious or personal beliefs, the candidate is led, phrase by phrase, through a terrible blood oath never to reveal the secrets of the Lodge.[16]

The *true* attitude of Freemasonry toward the Catholic Church is not to be learned from self-serving statements of

---

13. Albert Pike, *Morals and Dogma* (Richmond, VA: L.H. Jenkins, Inc. Edition Book Manufacturers, 1871; Mar. 1947 edition cited herein), p. 104.
14. Ibid., p. 109.
15. Ibid., p. 819.
16. Jim Shaw and Tom McKenney, *The Deadly Deception* (Lafayette, LA: Huntington House, Inc., 1988), pp. 25-26.

an ecumenical-sounding nature which one finds on occasion in the media, but rather from the ritual and oaths required from those entering the Thirtieth Degree of the Scottish Rite, Knights Kadosh, of which one part is the stabbing and trampling of a mock papal tiara to the shouts of "Down with imposture!"[17]

The Church is accused of having an insatiable thirst for power, of claiming despotism over the soul, of having sold absolutions, of decimating Europe to get rid of heretics, of decimating the Americas to convert Mexicans and Peruvians, and of seeking to subjugate the wills of others and to capture their souls, which is said to be at the bottom of all its proselytizing.[18]

Through its doctrines, Freemasonry continues to undermine all religion by claiming that a) religion can hope to attract the masses *only* by deliberately ladening itself with error;[19] b) God deliberately leads most people away from truth;[20] c) Christ is not divine;[21] d) Satan is not evil.[22]

Time and again, as we see in *Morals and Dogma*, Freemasonry hearkens back to the ancient pagan religions of India, Persia, Egypt and Greece, presenting them as the sources of true wisdom and light. It presents the "later" religions of Judaism and Christianity as setting up obstacles to "recovering" this "true" ancient wisdom—disregarding the fact that Christianity goes back, through the Israelites, to Adam's relationship with God at the very dawn of creation and that monotheism is the original religion of mankind. Just one result of this view is that the name of Jesus is never invoked in prayer in Masonic rituals—indeed it is forbidden

---

17. Paul A. Fisher, *Behind the Lodge Door* (Bowie, M.D.: Shield Pub. Co., 1988; Rockford, IL: TAN, 1991 & 1994), p. 240.
18. *Morals and Dogma*, p. 74.
19. Ibid., p. 224.
20. Ibid., p. 105.
21. Ibid., pp. 308, 524-525.
22. Ibid., pp. 102, 859.

to do so—and when the New Testament is quoted in these rituals, the name of Jesus must always be carefully excised.[23]

In our country, over a long period of time, Freemasonry has had a devastating influence in reinterpreting the U.S. Constitution such as to remove systematically or to restrict religion (particularly Christianity) and religious influence in many institutions of our society. For three decades, 1940-1970, the U.S. Supreme Court was dominated by Freemasons, and it was during this period that so many court decisions inimical to religion were written.[24]

One of the great ironies of this period is that many laws and practices directed against black Americans were struck down by a Supreme Court, most of whose members belonged to Freemasonry, which explicitly excludes blacks! *Separate and unequal* is the watchword for Freemasonry. While there is the Prince Hall system of Masonry for blacks, it is *not* considered authentic.[25] Freemasonry's support for the Ku Klux Klan is almost forgotten today, yet these two racist and anti-Catholic secret societies worked hand-in-glove for years.[26]

The role of Freemasonry in secularizing education in Europe and severely restricting the Church on that continent in the last two centuries is well known. This de-Christianizing of European society opened wide the door for Fascism, Nazism and Communism to attain power. Freemasonry aided these movements in seizing power, although these movements in turn suppressed Masonic lodges.[27]

Though in this country the Masons will always deny any mission to be involved in plots,[28] they will nevertheless clearly express sympathy for others involved in such activities, while directing their criticism mainly at the latter's unwise tactics. An example of this is the history written in

---

23. *The Deadly Deception,* pp. 72, 76.
24. *Behind the Lodge Door,* pp. 1-17.
25. *The Deadly Deception,* p. 29.
26. *Behind the Lodge Door,* pp. 87-102.
27. Ibid., pp. 217-230.
28. *Morals and Dogma,* p. 153.

Morals and Dogma about the Knights Templar, their suppression, and subsequent attempts at revenge by their successors during the French Revolution.[29]

In 1981 a Masonic plot to take over the government of Italy was exposed, showing once again that little has changed since Pope Leo XIII warned of Freemasonry's subversive activities aimed at the State.[30]

No attempt has been made in this chapter to go into the elaborate symbolism found in Freemasonry; suffice it to say that this symbolism is an intricate part of the secrecy and deceit of the movement. We leave the details to the larger works cited in this book.

4. Fact: The Church's stance on Freemasonry continues unchanged

What is the Catholic Church's position on Freemasonry today? In the 1960's and 1970's a certain amount of confusion arose due to a looser interpretation of penalties for Catholics who became members and to a misguided ecumenism, both of which resulted in some Catholics joining Masonic lodges with the approval of some clergy. However, after the new Code of Canon Law was issued (1983), the Holy See clarified the canon on secret societies (canon 1374)—in which Freemasonry is not mentioned by name—by stating clearly that membership in the Masons is forbidden to all Catholics and that membership is a serious sin which automatically denies Holy Communion to any Catholic who joins them. (See p. 31 below). Local Bishops may not make exceptions to this rule, this not being within their competence.

Subsequently, the U.S. bishops declared Freemasonry irreconcilable with Catholicism—indeed, with any form of Christianity.[31]

---

29. Ibid., pp. 1-2, 814-824.
30. *Behind the Lodge Door*, pp. 21-22.
31. Ibid., pp. 201-202.

Chapter 2

Freemasonry's Religious Lures

In a constant effort to increase its acceptability to every segment of society, Freemasonry uses symbols, objects and beliefs which are both familiar to and held sacred by those it seeks to lure into its movement.

Fundamentally opposed both to the Jewish religion and to Christianity, Freemasonry seeks to lure Jews and Christians through pretended tolerance and by using whatever it can of these religions in its ceremonies and teachings. For example, the Torah, the Temple in Jerusalem and various symbols of Judaism are used to lure Jews. For Christians, the Holy Bible, the feast days of St. John the Baptist and St. John the Evangelist, and the Sacraments of Baptism and Holy Eucharist are used.

Before going into the way elements of Christianity are used by Freemasonry, the fundamental difference between Freemasonry on the one hand, and both Judaism and Christianity on the other must be delineated.

That fundamental difference can be expressed in one word—_monotheism._

Monotheism is the truth that there is but _one_ God. All other "gods" are the inventions of man, and ultimately, of

Satan. Freemasonry seeks to overthrow this truth by reviving the ancient mysteries of the pagan religions of Egypt, Babylon, Persia, Greece and Rome.[1]

Since Freemasonry considers itself superior to all religions, it has no compunction about using Christian elements for its own ends.

> For Masonry is no religion, nor does it presume to take the place of any religion, but only to inculcate those principles of pure morality which Reason reads on the pages of the great Book of Nature, and to teach those great primary truths on which all religions repose. *What edifice of faith and creed each brother builds upon that foundation* [emphasis added] we have no *right* to inquire, and therefore do not seek to inquire.[2]

How is the Bible used? A Christian entering Freemasonry is strongly encouraged to swear the Masonic oaths he takes on the Bible. (Jews swear on the Torah, Muslims on the Koran.)

> The Bible is an indispensable part of the furniture of a *Christian* Lodge, only because it is the sacred book of the Christian religion. . . . The obligation of the candidate is always to be taken on the sacred book or books of his religion, that he may deem it more solemn and binding . . .[3]

Quotations from the Bible are used extensively at times in books explaining Masonic teachings and rituals, but the context in which these Scripture passages are used makes it clear that Christ's teachings are subservient to the teachings of Freemasonry.[5]

The feasts of St. John the Baptist (June 24) and St. John

1. *The Deadly Deception*, p. 143; also, *Behind the Lodge Door*, pp. 271-275.
2. Charles P. McClenachan, 33°, *The Book of The Ancient and Accepted Scottish Rite* (New York: Macoy Publishing & Masonic Supply Co., 1885; 1914, Revised & Enlarged Ed.), p. 558.
3. *Morals and Dogma*, p. 11.
4. Ibid., pp. 540-541.

the Evangelist (December 27) are important to Freemasonry because they mark the summer and winter solstices, which were important to the ancient pagan religions.[5] Also, both Saints were adopted by Freemasonry as a means of concealing their gnostic doctrines. Albert Pike in his work, *Morals and Dogma*, quoting an unnamed opponent of Freemasonry, puts it this way:

> The Templars, like all other Secret Orders and Associations, had two doctrines, one concealed and reserved for the Masters, which was Johannism; the other public, which was the Roman Catholic. Thus they deceived the adversaries whom they sought to supplant. Hence Freemasonry . . . adopted Saint John the Evangelist as one of its patrons, and associating with him, in order not to arouse the supicions of Rome, Saint John the Baptist. . . .[6]

It would, therefore, be most fitting to invoke the intercession of these two Saints when trying to gain the conversion of anyone ensnared in Freemasonry!

The perversion of the Sacraments of Baptism and the Holy Eucharist is another means of supplanting Christianity with Freemasonry.

Masonic baptism is practiced primarily in Europe, but the ceremonial is included in its book of rites for the northern jurisdiction of the U.S. According to the ceremonial,

> Masonic baptism was instituted far more for the parents than for the children, while it affords each father an occasion for renewing his own obligations. He, also, by concurring in an act which impresses upon his child of his own sex, in advance, the character of Mason, and which gives it, of either sex, a right to the protection and careful guardianship of the Lodge, obliges himself of necessity to rear it in the principles of Freemasonry. . . . In our ceremony

---

5. Ibid., pp. 368, 595.
6. Ibid., pp. 817-818.

of Baptism we neither imitate nor have it in view to supply the place of any religious rite of any church. For baptism is not the exclusive property of religion. As the natural symbol of purification of the soul, it was used in the ancient mysteries and solemnities of India, Egypt, and Greece. . . . It was not imagined that the ceremony itself [Masonic baptism] had any healing virtue, or conferred holiness upon the recipient.[7]

It is well to recall here that although Freemasonry claims it is not a religion and does not desire to replace any religion, yet by clearly declaring itself the *foundation* on which all members are to build their own personal creeds, *Freemasonry in effect claims to be superior to all religions*—the true super-religion governing all the others. (See footnote 2 above.)

Thus, while claiming not to be a religion, Freemasonry uses prayers, excerpts from the Scriptures and symbols identical to those used in Christian Baptism: water, oil, salt, a white garment and sponsors called godparents who make promises on behalf of the infant.

Water is used by the Worshipful Master to wash the infant's left hand as a cleansing symbol of innocence and purity of heart, mimicking the use of baptismal water in Christian Baptism.

Oil is used in Masonic baptism to anoint the child with the Delta symbol, which symbolizes three names of the Supreme Deity among the Syrians, the Phoenicians and the Hebrews (Self Existence, the Nature-God or Soul of the Universe, Supreme Power) in imitation of the anointing in the name of the Blessed Trinity in Christian Baptism.

Salt is placed on the tongue of the godfather and the infant in Masonic baptism as a symbol of the vow taken to watch over the infant. (In the traditional rite of Catholic Baptism, salt is blessed and used as a prayer for and symbol of the

---

7. *The Book of The Ancient and Accepted Scottish Rite*, pp. 557-558.

wisdom that preserves the baptized from the corruption of
sin, and as a protection against demonic influences in the
exorcism portion of the rite).

In Masonic baptism the infant is clothed in a white apron
as an emblem signifying that every Mason is destined for an
active and laborious life. The white garment in Christian
Baptism signifies the Christian dignity and state of grace of
the newly baptized child as a redeemed and sanctified child
of God. He is told that he must bring this garment of innocence and grace unstained into everlasting life.

Masonic godparents are the special instruments through
which the Lodge watches over and protects—until they are
adults (especially if they are orphaned)—the children of
Freemasons. In the traditional Catholic rite of Baptism,
Christian godparents, on behalf of the child, and speaking
for it, renounce Satan and all his works, profess the Faith
and vow to live the life of a good Christian. (This is done
by the parents in the new rite.)

It is obvious that the use of so many elements of Catholic
Baptism by Freemasonry is no innocent coincidence![8]

Just as Freemasonry uses the symbols of the Sacrament
of Baptism to its own ends, so also it mimics the Holy
Eucharist. Its ceremonies for Holy Thursday are a kind of
memorial of the Last Supper, commemorating the loss to
death of a "Most Wise and Perfect Master"—a Christ
stripped of His divinity. Former 33rd-Degree Scottish Rite
Mason Rev. Jim Shaw, in his book *The Deadly Deception*,
describes the ceremony:

> On Thursday evening we gathered at our home Temple
> and dressed for the ceremony. It was always a most solemn
> occasion and seemed a little awesome, even to those who
> had done it many times.
> Dressed in long, black, hooded robes we marched in, sin-
> gle file, with only our faces partly showing and took our seats.

8. Ibid., pp. 555-576. Also, *The Rites of the Catholic Church*, pp. 214-226.

There was something very tomb-like about the setting. . . . After the opening prayer (from which the name
of Jesus Christ was conspicuously excluded), I stood and
opened the service. As I had done so many times before,
I said, "We meet this day, to commemorate the death of
our 'Most Wise and Perfect Master,' not as inspired or
divine, for this is not for us to decide, but as at least the
greatest of the apostles of mankind. . . ."[9]

Rev. Shaw then goes on to describe the Masonic communion service, during which bread and wine are distributed
to the participants in a setting he describes as one of heavy
gloom, with its Christless prayers and hymns. He calls it a
Black Communion, a strange Black Mass. The service closes
with the snuffing out of candles, the last one representing
the life of Jesus: "We had dramatized and commemorated
the snuffing out of the life of Jesus, *without once mentioning
his name*, and the scene ended with the room in deep silent
darkness."[10]

These are just a few examples of elements taken from
Christianity, twisted around to fit Freemasonry's purposes,
which, because of their surface similarity to Christianity, can
lure the poorly instructed or nominal Christian into the
world of Freemasonry. Once in, he can be led, step by step,
away from Christ, the God-man and Redeemer, into a world
view where God and His teachings are systematically
blasphemed.

---

9. *The Deadly Deception*, pp. 105-106.
10. Ibid., p. 107.

Chapter 3

A Religion of Blasphemy

Freemasonry lays great store in the importance of *reason* in its belief system. In such a system, therefore, one would expect to find consistency as an integral feature. However, *inconsistency* is the hallmark of Freemasonry, for contradictions in it abound. Among the most notable is its claim both that it *is* and *is not* a religion.

> Every Masonic Lodge is a temple of religion; and its teachings are instruction in religion.[1]

> It is the universal, eternal, immutable religion, such as God planted it in the heart of universal humanity. No creed has ever been long-lived that was not built on this foundation.[2]

> Masonry is not a religion. He who makes of it a religious belief, falsifies and denaturalizes it.[3]

> For Masonry is no religion, nor does it assume to take the place of any religion, but only to inculcate those principles of pure morality which Reason reads on the pages of the

---

1. *Morals and Dogma*, p. 213.
2. Ibid., p. 219.
3. Ibid., p. 161.

great Book of Nature, and to teach those great primary truths on which all religions repose.[4]

The inconsistencies, the contradictions in the above quotations, which are so contrary to right reason, are obvious. There is one major aspect of Freemasonry that is hellishly consistent, however, and that is its systematic blasphemy against God and His Revelation to us through Holy Scripture and Sacred Tradition, handed down to us from the Apostles.

First of all, Freemasonry places itself *above* all divinely revealed religion (see the second and fourth quotations above). It also denies the divine inspiration and inerrancy of Sacred Scripture by declaring the books of the Bible to be merely a collection of oriental books of different ages, on a par with other ancient books,[5] and that the doctrines contained therein are not strict truth.[6]

God is portrayed as a deceiver who ". . . leads the masses away from the highest Truth,"[7] and as being merely, as man conceives Him, the reflected image of man himself,[8] which is the exact opposite of the truth, i.e., that we are made in the image and likeness of God. The Blessed Trinity becomes merely one in a series of "trinities" to be found in the various man-made pagan religions of old.[9]

Jesus Christ is portrayed as "Jesus of Nazareth," a great teacher whose teachings are quoted, but not as God, the Second Person of the Blessed Trinity: ". . . and every true Knight of the Rose will revere the memory of him who taught it, and look indulgently even on those who assign to him a character far above his own conception or belief, even to the

---

4. *The Book of The Ancient and Accepted Scottish Rite*, p. 558 (Ceremony of Baptism).
5. *Morals and Dogma*, p. 818.
6. Ibid., p. 224.
7. Ibid., p. 105.
8. Ibid., p. 223.
9. Ibid., pp. 548-563.

extent of deeming him Divine."[10] Even on Holy Thursday, when Christ is commemorated at Lodge services, Christ's name is omitted, and He is not prayed to; indeed, that is forbidden.[11]

The occult philosophies of ancient times are portrayed in a positive light, and magic is portrayed as a form of science, which ignorant Christianity suppressed by substituting faith for science.

> "The dunces who led primitive Christianity astray, by substituting faith for science . . . have succeeded in shrouding in darkness the ancient discoveries of the human mind."[12]

By denigrating faith in this fashion, in one fell swoop Freemasonry sweeps away belief in Christ, in His Church and its teachings, in the efficacy of the Mass and Sacraments and in Holy Scripture.

Satan's very existence is denied: ". . . there is no rebellious demon of Evil, or Principle of Darkness co-existent and in eternal controversy with God. . . ."[13] Satan is a force, not a person, created for good, but which may serve for evil, an instrument of liberty or free will.[14] Evil is portrayed as created by God,[15] and what we know as the effects of Original Sin on man were the intention of God for man.[16]

Freemasonry portrays itself as a friend and benefactor of all mankind, but its beliefs about humanity betray an underlying contempt of the human race and an elitism which admits only a relative few to knowledge of "Truth."[17] Mankind is portrayed as no better than the animals.[18] Free-

10. Ibid., p. 310.
11. *The Deadly Deception*, pp. 106, 136.
12. *Morals and Dogma*, p. 732.
13. Ibid., p. 859.
14. Ibid., p. 102.
15. *The Book of The Ancient and Accepted Scottish Rite*, p. 415.
16. Ibid., p. 416.
17. *Morals and Dogma*, pp. 104-105.
18. Ibid., p. 295.

masonry teaches that it is permissible for a "superior" race to rule an "inferior" one, and that God's justice ". . . does not require us to relieve the hard-working millions of all labor, to emancipate the serf or slave, unfitted to be free, from all control."[19]

In the following chapter we shall examine Freemasonry's similarity to the New Age Movement, which denies that Jesus Christ is God and which ultimately worships Satan.

At every turn one takes in the maze of Freemasonry, he runs up against a black wall of blasphemy. Indeed, that seems to be the reason for its existence—the establishment of a religion of blasphemy!

---

19. Ibid., p. 829.

Chapter 4

Partisans of Evil

In Chapter One we quoted extensively from Pope Leo XIII's encyclical *Humanum Genus* (1884) in order to lay the groundwork for considering modern-day Freemasonry.

We return to that encyclical in order to highlight in this chapter one of the important aspects of Freemasonry Pope Leo XIII pointed out over a century ago. Equating Freemasonry with the domain of Satan, using St. Augustine's image of the two cities, the City of man and the City of God, the Pope warned that there was a coming together of the "partisans of evil," led on in particular by Freemasonry.[1]

Now let us look at that phrase of Pope Leo XIII regarding the "partisans of evil" coming together and being led by Freemasonry. Pope Leo had warned that the Masons would abet socialist and Communist revolutions everywhere. Let us examine some history of this century.

By World War I, many European governments were dominated or heavily influenced by Freemasons. Catholic schools were closed and outlawed in some nations. In the aftermath of World War I, Communism seized control of Russia; a few years later Mussolini's black-shirted socialists, called Fascists, took over Italy; and in 1933 the Nazis, though receiving less

---

1. *Humanum Genus*, Pope Leo XIII, 1884, no. 2.

than 50% of the vote, formed a government in Germany and quickly suppressed all opposition. All of these were supported by Freemasons at the time.

Nazism (like Freemasonry and the New Age movement today) was riddled with occultism (the swastika is from ancient pagan religions). Among Nazis there was a fascination for ancient pagan religions of the East. Nazism also sought to revive interest in the ancient pagan religions of pre-Christian Germany, coupled with theories of racial purity and the superiority of Germans. Communism also has occultic roots. If some of Karl Marx's writings—including his poetry—are a barometer, he was a Satanist, not an atheist. So we can see that all these "isms" have a certain commonality. Fascism in Italy, used the pagan symbols of ancient Rome.

Of late, there seems to be an increasing awareness of a coming together of Communism and Freemasonry. In fact, the co-operation between Communism in the East and Freemasonry in the increasingly pagan West—with its secular humanist allies of the New Age movement—is becoming more unashamedly open. A number of instances can be cited in support of this view.

In July, 1990 Fr. Robert Bradley, S.J., at a Blue Army symposium in Washington, D.C., spoke of the connection between Our Lady's message at Fatima and Freemasonry. Though her message is known chiefly for its warning on Communism, Father Bradley makes the case that Mary was clearly advising us about Freemasonry, although neither evil is mentioned specifically by name.

The welcome temporary respite from five decades of totalitarian rule now being experienced in some parts of Eastern Europe has also been accompanied by an influx of Western materialism and the reconstitution of Lodges of Freemasonry throughout that region. In *30 DAYS* magazine (July-August 1990 issue), in a piece accompanying an article on the statement of the Bishops of the Indian Ocean Episcopal Conference on the dangers of Freemasonry, we find a short review of the attempts to reactivate Masonic Lodges throughout Eastern Europe and the U.S.S.R.[2] This was prior to the dramatic events of 1991.

In its September-October 1990 issue, *30 DAYS* ran a five-page article, "From Communism to Masonry," giving extensive treatment to the resurgence of Freemasonry in Eastern Europe and the U.S.S.R., as well as historical background on Freemasonry's past in each country. Indeed, a resurgent Evil Empire is in the making![3]

Even though the source is a private revelation—which we are not required to accept—it may be worth noting that the 1990 edition of *To The Priests,* by Don Stefano Gobbi of the Marian Movement of Priests, contains several reported locutions from Our Lady explaining some aspects of the Book of Revelation (the *Apocalypse*) concerning the Red Dragon (atheistic Communism) and the black beast arising from the sea (Freemasonry) and the work of both in promoting apostasy and idolatry. It is said that the two will reach their zenith by 1998.[4]

A book published in 1990 by A. Ralph Epperson, *The New World Order,* drawing extensively on Masonic and New Age movement sources, shows the similarities and interplay between these two movements in this country and their efforts to replace America's Judaeo-Christian heritage with a brutal form of paganism, leading ultimately to the worship of Lucifer and the elimination of every vestige of Christianity.[5]

This interplay between Freemasonry and the New Age movement consists in their common views and in what they advocate—but not in their structures. Freemasonry is highly structured. It is a male-only organization, hierarchical, with very precise, elaborate rituals. It has separate groups for

---

2. *30 DAYS*, July-August 1990, p. 29.
3. Ibid., September-October 1990, pp. 60-64.
4. Don Stefano Gobbi, *To the Priests, Our Lady's Beloved Sons,* 1990, pp. 641-656. This book carries the *Imprimatur* of the Most Rev. James J. Byrne, STD, retired Archbishop of Dubuque.
5. A. Ralph Epperson, *The New World Order* (Publius Press, Tucson, AZ, 1990).

women and children, which are closely monitored by the male members who oversee them.

On the other hand, the New Age movement is an apparently headless network of many groups, interacting in such a way as to build a New World Order in which monotheistic religions, such as Christianity and Judaism, with their "restrictive" or "unhealthy" moral codes, will have to change drastically or be abolished (by force, if necessary). Christianity and Judaism impede the "progress" that the New Agers seeks to make.

The New Age has what it calls "the Christ," but this "Christ" is NOT the Christ of the Gospels, i.e., Jesus Christ, True God and True Man, the Second Person of the Blessed Trinity. In the New Age view, Jesus is *separate* from Christ; Jesus is a great *man*, like Buddha or Confucius, but is not God—He is simply a *way* to "the Christ." *It is this view of Christ that New Agers want Christians to adopt.* They want to *change* Christianity! Again, they separate *Jesus* from *Christ!* St. John the Evangelist had already faced this blasphemy back in the first century. He wrote, "Who is a liar, but he who denieth that Jesus is the Christ? This is Antichrist, who denieth the Father, and the Son. (*1 John* 2:22).

What are some of the elements common to Freemasonry and the New Age?

Both seek "Light." But when all is said and done, that "light" turns out to be Lucifer. Both deny the existence of divinely revealed religion. Both denigrate Sacred Scripture by denying its inerrancy and divine inspiration, and consider the Scriptures as merely a collection of sacred books written by men. Both deny Jesus Christ's divinity and His role as Saviour and Redeemer, as well as the fact that He established a Church. Both promote a "secret wisdom" to be gleaned from the ancient pagan religions of the East. Both promote astrology and reincarnation. Both have a gnosticism, with its elitist mentality and the lure of a secret knowledge and wisdom (which not everyone should be privy to) as the core of their beliefs. Ultimately both will lead into the worship of Satan, though many in both movements—probably the vast majority—do not realize this!

It seems that, given its much longer existence, Freemasonry has, over the past century, spawned the creation of the New Age movement as a means to spread its beliefs among that great majority of people who would never otherwise be "evangelized," if you will, by Freemasonry's highly structured regular organization. At some point in time, this link might be openly revealed by Masonry's leaders.

Let us examine a little further just a couple of the elements common to Freemasonry and the New Age. Belief in reincarnation is quite popular in our country today. It is an *integral* part of the New Age movement, and it is *clearly* central to Freemasonry. J. D. Buck (32nd° Mason), a still well-respected Masonic author of the 1920's, wrote the following in his book, *Symbolism of Freemasonry or Mystic Masonry and the Greater Mysteries of Antiquity* (1925), regarding those who help the poor:

> Reincarnation being true, these servants of humanity are laying by a store of good Karma, which is literally, "treasure in heaven," and which must inevitably secure for them still broader opportunities and greater power for good in another life; and best of all, they are unfolding the higher spiritual perceptions. (P. 9).

Following is another quote from the same author regarding salvation and Christ. In essence, the Masonic author repeats the serpent's old lie that we can be our own gods, our own saviours—thus, we do not need Jesus Christ. Then the author claims that this (obviously perverted) notion was taught by the early Church! Again, one will also find this same type of thinking in the New Age movement today:

> Every soul must "work out its own salvation" and "take the Kingdom of Heaven by force." Salvation by faith and

Freemasonry—Mankind's Hidden Enemy

the vicarious atonement were not taught, as now interpreted, by Jesus, nor are these doctrines taught in the exoteric Scriptures. They are later and ignorant perversions of the original doctrines. In the early Church, as in the Secret Doctrine, there was not one Christ for the whole world, but a *potential* Christ in every man. Theologians first made a fetish of the Impersonal, Omnipresent Divinity; and then tore the *Christos* from the hearts of all humanity in order to deify Jesus; that they might have a God-man peculiarly their own! (P. 57).

Because of Original Sin, the human heart feels very tempted by the blasphemous ideal of being its own god. But to follow that path is to forfeit the true sharing in Divine Life through Jesus Christ. The attempt to be one's own god and saviour ends in everlasting death.

Today more than ever we see the truth of St. Maximilian Kolbe's words: "Modern times are dominated by Satan and will be more so in the future. The conflict with Hell cannot be engaged by men, even the most clever. The Immaculata alone has from God the promise of victory over Satan."

And what has been Mary Immaculate's advice to us, time and again? Attendance at Mass, frequent use of the Sacraments, daily prayer (especially the Rosary), love, obedience to and prayer for the Pope, the offering up of the sacrifices of our daily lives well-lived, and total consecration to her Immaculate Heart.

We need to keep our eyes fixed on Christ our Saviour, our hands in Mary's hands, our ears attuned to the voice of Peter, and to have the wisdom and courage to be narrow-minded enough to tune out all contrary voices. All Scripture from *Genesis* to the *Apocalypse (Revelation)* assures us of the triumph of the City of God over the city of man. The grandiose schemes and machinations of the partisans of evil of our era are ultimately doomed to failure. We need but to stay our course!

Chapter 5

Masons and Mafias

Since this book was first published (1995), information on another aspect of Freemasonry has come to light. It concerns the connections between Masons belonging to European Orient lodges and powerful, highly organized bands of criminals dealing in drugs, guns, money-laundering and extensive political corruption.

The information on this aspect of Freemasonry is from British author Brian Freemantle's book *The Octopus*, which exposes the activities of organized crime in the European Union and its member nations. Freemantle labels these gangs "mafias" (with a small "m")—a generic term he uses to describe organized crime gangs in Europe. These gangs include the Sicilian Costa Nostra,* whence the word *mafia* originated. The Sicilian mafia is but one part of the whole system of present-day mafias.

The author makes the point that the Orient Masonic lodges connected with these mafias are considered "outlaw" or "irregular" lodges by the British Masonic lodges, which supposedly are the supreme authority in Freemasonry, though that supreme authority has had no noticeable effect on the Orient lodges' criminal activities.

The overall thrust of Freemantle's book is to portray the very real danger of organized crime's becoming capable of

---

*Costa Nostra—more commonly called the *Cosa Nostra*.

completely dominating the European continent. One very significant element in this situation is the enormous power and influence of Orient Freemasonry within this system of European organized crime. In both the lodges and the mafias, blood oaths of secrecy are essential to the organizations' activities. Freemantle puts it this way: "The secrecy rituals of the Orient Freemasons are more symbolic than the literal death-for-dishonor oaths of the Costa Nostra, but the secrecy is nevertheless meticulously maintained by European Masons, in both east and west. This makes each the perfect blood brother for the other, and provides secure shell-within-a-shell concealment for both."[1]

Italy is cited as a prime example of how a nation's government and democratic institutions can be subverted and destroyed by this powerful masonic-mafia crime combine—a partnership which now threatens the entire supranational European Union. For example, although the Propaganda Due (P2) Lodge's attempt to overthrow the Italian government in 1981 was thwarted and the names of over 900 members were revealed, most of that lodge's membership was never exposed, and these members have continued to operate as a secret lodge to this day, along with other newer secret lodges formed since then. By the 1990s, the Italian political system had blown apart; the major political parties were destroyed by scandal after scandal—which in turn exposed the corrupt and criminal actions of party leaders and officeholders (from Prime Ministers on down), including bribes and extortion paid by all kinds of business enterprises.

Another component of the Masonic-mafia crime partnership is its international money-laundering apparatus. These money-laundering operations go on in banks and corporations (some of them established solely for this purpose) all over the world from Hong Kong to Switzerland to Panama to Monaco and various island nations scattered throughout the

---

1. Brian Freemantle, *The Octopus*, (Orion Books, Ltd., Orion House, 5 Upper St. Martin's Lane, London, England WC2H 9EA, 1995), p. 11.

Caribbean and the Pacific. The Vatican Bank scandal of the 1980s was but one episode.

In Eastern Europe too, the Masonic-mafia crime partnership has put down deep roots. Citing Leoluca Orlando, the founder of Italy's anti-mafia party and now a member of the European Union Parliament, Freemantle writes: "Always, too, criminals and Masons work together. Leoluca Orlando insisted during our meeting, 'In Eastern Europe there is a very strong masonry and there is a very strong mafia and they are very big together.' So much money was being laundered in the former Communist countries, in Orlando's opinion, that organized crime was actually going beyond buying up banks to buying up parts of the various states. 'The investment in Eastern Europe will be the biggest money-cleansing operation in the history of humanity.' "[2]

The enormous amount of influence these gangs have attained within the institutions of the European Union is astounding. Huge sums of money have been stolen or used as bribes or for political favor trading, such as various agricultural subsidies. European Union officials often simply refuse to acknowledge the problem, as the Masonic-mafia crime duo continues to trade concessions at the highest levels of both the Union and its participating governments. Its agents have been successfully inserted into key positions of the European Union for many years and are able to secure "suitable" replacements for those whose tenure expires.

Since there are such clearly demonstrated links between Masonry and organized crime in Europe, the question must be raised: Are there similar links between Masonry and organized crime in the Western Hemisphere?

We already know that money-laundering operations span the globe and that the banks involved launder money from drug kingpins in the U.S., Mexico, Colombia, etc. Given the Masons' decades-long influence within Mexico's government,

---

2. Ibid., p. 72.

is there not a good chance of links between crime and Masonry in that country? Repeatedly, Mexican officials responsible for uprooting drug trafficking are proved to be in cahoots with Mexican drug kingpins.

What about the United States? Our wealth and influence target us as the biggest plum of all. Certainly the U.S. has not been immune to drug-running, gun-running, money-laundering, or to the buying and selling of political influence at every level and branch of government!

Freemasons here (like those in Britain) have always denied that the U.S. suffers from any form of the machinations and political plots that occur in Europe. Yet it must be pointed out that in the early decades of this century, Masons in this country were extensively involved with the then politically powerful Knights of the Ku Klux Klan, when those hooded hoodlums were riding high throughout the land.

To date there has been no hint of Masonic ties to organized crime in the U.S.—but was there any hint of such ties in Italy before the Propaganda Due exposé in 1981?

Appendices

Including Current
Official Catholic Statements

Appendix A

Knights of the Immaculata vs. Freemasonry's Poison

By St. Maximilian Kolbe

NOTE: *In an early account of his founding of the* Militia Immaculatae [*Knights of the Immaculata*], *St. Maximilian Kolbe related how as a boy of about 14 he one day bowed his head to the floor while praying in the friars' choir in the Order's minor seminary in Lwów, Poland. There he made the suprising promise to the Immaculata that he would fight for her. He does not say so explicitly, but he hints that he made this promise in response to her direct request, probably in a vision or an apparition. He states that at the time he had no idea as to how he would do this.*

The answer came years later, in 1917 in Rome, when the Freemasons were noisily celebrating their second centenary with bold demonstrations in the streets, proclaiming the coming destruction of the Church. These crystallized in the young student friar's mind what exactly the Immaculata wanted him to fight for, as he explains in the following article written in 1939.—Fr. Bernard Geiger, O.F.M. Conv., Translator.

Before the World War [WWI], in Rome, the capital city of Christian life, the secret society of the Freemasons was growing daily more aggressive, in spite of the fact that the

Popes very often exposed and condemned it. These Freemasons were not even afraid to march around on Giordano Bruno's anniversary, carrying black banners depicting the Archangel Michael being trodden underfoot by Satanic Lucifer, as he is called, or to flaunt Masonic insignia beneath the very windows of the Vatican. Some enraged hands dared to write such slogans as "Satan will rule on Vatican Hill, and the Pope will serve as his errand boy," and other such insults. Now these unreasoning acts of hatred toward the Church of Christ and His temporal Vicar were not the inept rantings of a few individual psychopaths, but the manner, way and plan of action deduced from the Masonic rule: Destroy all teaching about God, especially Catholic teaching.

Destroy Catholicism by Corrupting Morals

Centers of this secret society have been established in every region. Nevertheless, in various ways they more or less openly promote one and the same thing. In their plan, they use many and various kinds of socities which, under their leadership, promote neglect of divine things and the breakdown of morality. This is because the Freemasons follow this principle above all: *"Catholicism can be overcome not by logical argument but by corrupted morals."* [Emphasis added]. And so they overwhelm the souls of men with the kind of literature and arts that will most easily destroy a sense of chaste morals, and they foster sordid lifestyles in all phases of human life. As a result, the once-strong characters of men are weakened, families are broken up by guilt-laden hearts, and an unhealthy sorrowfulness continues to grow. When such perons are unable to shake off the miserable yoke they carry, they avoid the Church and even rise up against her. To bring help to so many unhappy persons, to stabilize innocent hearts, so that all can more easily go to the Immaculate Virgin, through whom so many graces come down to us, the *Militia Immaculatae* (Knights of the Immaculata movement) was established in Rome in 1917 in the International College of the Friars Minor Conventual.

Appendix B

Declaration on Masonic Associations

By the Sacred Congregation for the
Doctrine of the Faith
November 26, 1983

It has been asked whether the position of the Church in regard to Freemasonry has been changed by reason of the fact that there is no express mention of the same in the New Code of Canon Law [1983], as there was in the previous Code [1917].

This Congregation is able to reply that the circumstance indicated is due to an editorial policy which has been followed in regard to other associations as well, which have likewise not been mentioned, inasmuch as they are included in broader categories.

For this reason, therefore, the negative position of the Church in regard to Masonic associations remains unchanged, since their basic principles have always been considered irreconcilable with the teachings of the Church, and consequently, membership in them remains forbidden. The faithful who belong to Masonic associations are in a state of grave sin and may not receive Holy Communion.

It is not within the competence of local [diocesan] church

authorities to pass judgment on the nature of Masonic associations in such a way as to derogate from what has been established above; this is in line with the Declaration of this Congregation issued February 17, 1981. (Cf. *Acts of the Apostolic See*, 723/1981, pp. 240-241.)

The Supreme Pontiff, John Paul II, in the course of the audience granted to the undersigned Cardinal Prefect, approved the present Declaration, which was decided upon in the [previous] ordinary meeting of this Sacred Congregation, and has ordered its publication.

Rome, from the office of the Sacred Congregation for the Doctrine of the Faith, November 26, 1983.

> Joseph Cardinal Ratzinger
>   Prefect
> Fr. Jérome Hamer, O.P.
>   Titular Archbishop of Lorium
>   Secretary

(*L'Osservatore Romano*, November 27, 1983, p. 2. Translated from the Italian by Fr. Bernard M. Geiger, O.F.M. Conv.)

Appendix C

Masonry and Naturalistic Religion

Statement of the U.S. Bishops' Committee
For Pastoral Research and Practices
Released April 19, 1985

I. History of the Masons' Situation

Recently [November 26, 1983] the Congregation for the Doctrine of the Faith responded to an inquiry whether the Church's position regarding Masonic organizations has been altered, especially since no explicit mention is made of them in the New Code of Canon Law [1983], as there was in the Old Code [1917].

The Congregation stated that the Masons and other organizations were omitted in the New Code due to a different criterion adopted in drafting the code. They were included in broader categories. [See Canon 1374.] The Congregation did not, however, specify the categories it had in mind (it might have been thinking of such canons as Canon 1364), but it insisted that the Church is still opposed to Masonic associations, since their principles are irreconcilable with the Church's doctrine and that it would be seriously wrong to join them.

In the Old Code an excommunication was incurred by those who joined the Masons or other organizations *that plotted against the Church or legitimate civil authority.*

In a response given by Cardinal Seper in 1974 regarding the force and meaning of Canon 2335, it was stated that the canon still remained in force but that, since penal laws are subject to strict interpretation, the penalty would be incurred in a particular case only by those who join associations which plot against the Church. If the particular organization did not plot against the Church, the excommunication would not be incurred by the person who joined them.

This was interpreted by some bishops to mean that it was permissible to join the Masons if the particular organization did not plot against the Church, etc.

In 1981, since the previous letter had "given rise to erroneous and tendentious interpretations," the Congregation for the Doctrine of the Faith affirmed the current (at that time) canonical discipline, and while still admitting a strict interpretation of the penalty, denied any intention of remanding to bishops' conferences the making of public pronouncements of a general nature on the nature of Masonic associations, etc. But since the Congregation spoke in the context of the Old Code (Canon 2335), it is not entirely relevant today.

The whole issue came into sharper focus with the advent of the New Code and the absence of a censure for joining organizations that plotted against the Church. The response of the Congregation for the Doctrine of the Faith on November 26, 1983, was to this issue.

What is at stake is the distinction between penal law and morality. There is a difference between the two. Not everything that is immoral is penalized in the Church. Nor can one conclude from the fact that penal law does not cover some sin or that it is removed from it (or changed), that it is permissible to commit it. A clear example of this is abortion. Even if the excommunication were removed from abortion, it would still be wrong. Similarly, even if the excommunication were removed from joining an organization that plotted against the Church, it would still be wrong to join such an organization.

Moreover, even if the Masons did not plot against the Church, it might be seriously wrong to join them for other reasons. The Congregation presents as the reason for its judgment the fact that the principles of Masonry are "irreconcilable" with those of the Church. The six-year study of Masonry by the German bishops and the study of American Masonry by Professor William Whalen (commissioned by the Pastoral Research and Practices Committee) both confirm that the principles and basic rituals of Masonry embody a naturalistic religion, active participation in which is incompatible with Christian faith and practice. Those who knowingly embrace such principles are committing serious sin (they might also fall under the penalty in Canon 1364 in the New Code). Briefly, the conclusion is that even though there is no longer an excommunication attached to joining organizations that plot against the Faith, it would still be wrong to join such an organization. And even though Masonic organizations may not in particular cases plot against the Faith, it would still be wrong to join them because their basic principles are irreconcilable with those of the Catholic Faith.

II. Problems with the Masonic Question

The committee recognizes two problems in regard to the Masonic question:

1. A pastoral problem for those who have become or continue to be Masons in good faith on the basis of the less-restrictive interpretation which followed the Congregation for the Doctrine of the Faith's letter to Cardinal Krol. It is the question of applying the traditional principles for leaving them in good faith.

2. A public-relations problem resulting from the common American perception of Masonry as a purely social and philanthropic organization.

(With permission of U.S. Bishops' Committee for Pastoral Research and Practices. Origins, June 27, 1985, p. 83ff.)

Appendix D

The Pastoral Problem of Masonic Membership

Professor William Whalen's Report for the Bishops' Committee for Pastoral Research and Practices, Released Along with the Committee's own Statement.

Modern speculative Freemasonry began in 1717 with the establishment in London of the Grand Lodge of England. A little more than two decades later, Clement XII forbade Catholic membership in these lodges, and the opposition of the Catholic Church has been restated by seven other popes.

The most recent statement was given by the Congregation for the Doctrine of the Faith, November 26, 1983. In part it declared, "The Church's negative position on Masonic associations, therefore, remains unaltered, since their principles have always been regarded as irreconcilable with the Church's doctrine." The document added that "Catholics enrolled in Masonic associations are involved in serious sin and may not approach Holy Communion."

This paper will examine the reasons for the historical and present position of the Church vis-a-vis Freemasonry and will do so in the American context. We should understand that, worldwide, Freemasonry shares many beliefs and customs, but is not a unified organization; it includes the United

Grand Lodge of England; the fifty independent grand lodges in the United States; lodges in Canada, Australia and New Zealand; Prince Hall Masonry; the so-called Christian Masonry of Germany and the three Scandinavian countries; the various Grand Orients of Europe and Latin America; co-Masonic bodies; irregular lodges, such as the Italian P2 Lodge; and others.

Pastoral Problem Due to Misunderstanding

That the Church has for centuries condemned Freemasonry and excommunicated Catholics who joined the Lodge, or refused Baptism to those who declined to sever their Lodge affiliations, is clear. That the Church today considers Masonic membership serious enough to deny the Eucharist to "Catholic Masons" is also clear. What has created a pastoral problem in some dioceses is that for a period of some years membership by the laity in Masonic Lodges seemed to be an option. From 1974 to 1981, and even beyond, an undetermined number of Catholic men joined the Lodge, and many of them retain their membership. Articles in the Catholic press told readers that under certain circumstances such membership was now allowed. The general public, Catholic and non-Catholic, got the impression that the Church had softened its stand against membership in Freemasonry.

We will examine the major reasons why the Church has taken the attitude it has since the mid-eighteenth century and why these reasons justify the present position. But first, we should take a brief look at the documents which created the recent confusion.

Cardinal Franjo Seper, then prefect of the Congregation for the Doctrine of the Faith, sent a letter dated July 19, 1974, to Cardinal John Krol, which concluded that "Canon 2335 regards only those Catholics who join associations which plot against the Church." Even if it were determined that a particular Masonic association did not plot against the Church, membership was still forbidden to clerics, religious and members of secular institutes.

Presumably the local ordinary was expected to conduct an investigation to see whether a particular secret society in his diocese was engaged in a plot against the Church. Cardinal Seper's letter made no reference to the traditional objections to Freemasonry, namely, its religious naturalism and its oaths. Nor did the letter suggest a methodology by which a bishop might conduct his investigation, in view of the fact that the members of the Lodge, like members of the Irish Republican Army, the Mafia and other secret organizations, were sworn to secrecy.

As late as October 1984, a nationally syndicated columnist for the Catholic press was assuring his readers that Catholics "may indeed hold membership in organizations, Masonic and otherwise, which are not basically anti-Catholic and do not plot against the Church." The columnist told his readers that "direction and guidance concerning the various organizations in your own locality can easily be obtained from the chancery office of your diocese." Would that it were so. At the very least one would suppose that anyone professing minimum expertise in the area of Freemasonry would have studied the ritual of the Lodge, as well as basic Masonic sources, such as Pike's *Morals and Dogma*, [and also] *Humanum Genus* by Leo XIII and such criticisms as Father Walton Hannah's *Darkness Visible* and *Christian by Degrees* and Whalen's *Christianity and American Freemasonry.* One wonders how many people in the typical chancery have spent even this amount of time on the question so that they could answer inquirers' questions with confidence.

Some bishops evidently conducted such investigations, or perhaps decided they had no way of determining the character of a particular secret society, and allowed Catholic men in their dioceses to join the Lodges. Other bishops denied requests to join.

A clarification from the Congregation was published March 2, 1981. It referred to "erroneous and tendentious interpretations" of the "confidential letter" of July 19, 1974. The clarification affirmed that the present canonical discipline had not been modified in any way, that neither the excommunication nor other penalties had been abrogated and that it was not the intention of the Congregation "to remand to the bishops' conferences the making of public pronouncements with a judgment of a general nature on the nature of the Masonic associations, such as would imply the derogation of the aforesaid norms."

Canon 2335 of the 1917 Code of Canon Law had stated, "Those who join a Masonic sect or other societies of the same sort, which plot against the Church or against legitimate civil authority, incur excommunication." When the new Code of Canon Law was published, no mention was made of the traditional penalty of excommunication of Catholics who joined the Masonic Lodge.[1] Again the possibility of misunderstanding arose because the general public was not aware that the number of offenses for which excommunication was applied had been reduced from thirty-seven to seven. The 1981 clarification had received little publicity. Cardinal Joseph Ratzinger then issued the November 26, 1983 document, which reaffirmed the historic position against Freemasonry. This statement had also been specifically approved by John Paul II.

Reasons for Condemnation

The March 11, 1985 issue of *L'Osservatore Romano* carried an article titled "Irreconcilability Between Christian Faith and Freemasonry," as a comment on the November 26, 1983 declaration. In part, the Vatican newspaper said a Christian "cannot cultivate relations of two types with God nor express his relation with the Creator through symbolic forms of two types. That would be something completely different from that collaboration, which to him is obvious, with all those

---

1. Canon 1374 of the new Code of Canon Law (1983) states: "One who joins an association which plots against the Church is to be punished with a just penalty; one who promotes or moderates such an association, however, is to be punished with an interdict."—*Bro. C. M.*

who are committed to doing good, even if beginning from different principles. On the one hand, a Catholic Christian cannot at the same time share in the full communion of Christian brotherhood and, on the other, look upon his Christian brother, from the Masonic perspective, as an 'outsider.'"

Some have suggested that the reaffirmation of the historic condemnation by the Church was prompted by the P2 scandal. Grand Master Licio Gelli directed this secret Masonic Lodge known as Propaganda Due or P2, whose aim seems to have been to restore fascism in Italy and to bolster right-wing governments in Latin America. When Italian police raided his villa in 1981, they discovered the Lodge's membership roster, which listed 953 people, including the heads of Italy's intelligence agencies, generals, cabinet ministers, judges, bankers, industrialists and the like. Gelli had persuaded a number of individuals, such as financier Roberto Calvi, that membership in the Masonic Lodge was now allowed by the Church. Actually, it appears that the P2 Lodge plotted more against the Italian state than [against] the Church, although the Masonic financiers who were called in to handle the Vatican's investments (such as Sindona) cost the Church many millions of dollars. The P2 case did demonstrate that Masonic secrecy could camouflage and facilitate conspiracies of the political right, even in the shadows of St. Peter's.

On the other hand, a recent book by Stephen Knight alleges that the KGB used the secrecy and networking of English Freemasonry to place spies in top intelligence jobs. It encouraged its operatives to try to join Masonic Lodges to gain preferential treatment in their careers. In particular, the author charges that Freemasons propelled Sir Roger Hollis into a series of rapid promotions, which led to his being named head of M15 counterintelligence in 1956. A book by Chapman Pincher, published in 1981, attempted to prove that Hollis was a Soviet agent. Knight's book was published in the United States in November, 1984 by Stein and Day of New York under the title *The Brotherhood: The Secret World of Freemasons*.

Both the right and the left have seen the advantages of using the Masonic organizations to further their causes. At one time, Masonry was known as a chief bulwark of republican forms of governments. Actually, in the United States today most observers would probably label the Lodges as both politically reactionary and racist.

Although the 1981 clarification by the Sacred Congregation came shortly after the exposure of the P2 conspiracy, nothing in the statement indicated that its intent was limited to Italian or continental Masonry. An estimated 30,000 Masons belong to five hundred lodges within three jurisdictions in Italy. Everyone knows that the Grand Orient Lodges of Europe and Latin America have been anti-clerical from the start. For the Congregation for the Doctrine of the Faith to advise Catholics against joining these Grand Orient Lodges would be like the National Association for the Advancement of Colored People advising blacks against applying for membership in the Ku Klux Klan. Those who say that the Church really directs her condemnation against the Grand Orient Lodges must assume that the Vatican does not know that Freemasonry is English in origin and overwhelmingly English-speaking in membership. Of the estimated six million members in all the various types of Masonic Lodges worldwide, about four million live in the United States, 750,000 in the United Kingdom, 250,000 in Canada, and 400,000 in Australia and New Zealand. Perhaps nine out of ten Masons live in an English-speaking country.

For U.S. bishops and priests, the pastoral problem not only involves those Catholic laymen who joined Masonic lodges during the period of confusion in the late 1970s and early 1980s. It extends to the general public, Catholic and non-Catholic, which does not understand why the Catholic Church, in an era of ecumenism, persists in condemning an organization often known for its charities and good works. We have no reason to doubt the testimony of so many American Masons that they have never heard a word of criticism of the

Roman Church in lodge meetings or functions. In fact, Masonry rules out discussions of religion and politics in the Lodge.

Masonic Stands, Ritual and Principles

We should understand that Masonry basically consists of the three degrees of the Blue Lodge: entered apprentice, fellow craft and master Mason. The Lodges are grouped in independent grand lodges in the fifty states.

If he wishes, a master Mason may elect to continue his Masonic career by entering the so-called higher degrees: The Scottish or the York (or American) rite. (Jews are, however, barred from the York rite). Membership in the Scottish rite leads to the 32nd degree and the honorary 33rd degree. The fourth to the 32nd degrees are ordinarily conferred on a class over a weekend in a Scottish-rite cathedral; in Europe the candidate must spend many years to reach the 32nd degree, which is another contrast between the mass Masonry in the United States and the elite Masonry of the Continent. The goal of all those who choose to go up the York-rite ladder is membership in the Knights Templar. Both 32nd degree Scottish-rite Masons and Knights Templar are eligible to join the Shrine, which serves as the playground of American Masonry and supports notable charitable institutions, such as its hospitals for crippled children. Father Hannah called its pseudo-Islamic ritual the "adolescent and occasionally Rabelaisian nadir of drivelling tomfoolery and burlesque blasphemies." English Freemasonry would never tolerate an organization such as the Shrine, but obviously hundreds of thousands of U.S. Masons find in the Shrine the fun they do not find in the teetotalling, sober Blue Lodges.

Many other organizations require Masonic membership, but they do not form an integral part of Freemasonry. These include the Grotto, Square and Compass Clubs, National Sojourners, High Twelve clubs, Tall Cedars of Lebanon, etc. A Mason who quits or is expelled from his Blue Lodge forfeits membership in any other Masonic organizations. Attendance requirements are unknown in the Blue Lodge, so that simple payment of dues keeps members in good standing.

If the American Blue Lodges are not especially anti-Catholic, the religious neutrality of an organization such as the Southern jurisdiction of the Scottish rite, which enrolls 600,000 Masons in thirty-three Southern and Western states, is another matter. The hostility of this group to parochial schools remains unabated and readers of the *New Age* [magazine] are well aware of the attitude of the Southern jurisdiction to Roman Catholicism.

In a 1978 article in the *Review of Religious Research*, two (non-Catholic) scholars examined "Fraternal Associations and Civil Religion: Scottish-rite Freemasonry." Among many observations the authors noted:

> In their support of civil religion, the Masons are militantly "anti-particularistic," to use Sidney Mead's term. They vigorously denounce parochial schools for challenging the public school system and, implicitly, the unifying civil religion. Sectarian religion has positive values, but it is relegated to the sphere of private morality and private faith. (Pamela M. Jolicoeur and Louis L. Knowles, Vol. 20, No. 1, Fall 1978, pp. 13-14).

Those who direct the Scottish rite, Southern jurisdiction, would be delighted if every parochial school closed tomorrow. This may not technically involve a plot against the Church, but it raises the question of allowing, much less encouraging, Catholics in these Southern and Western states to participate in the Scottish rite.

If anti-Catholicism and racism in U.S. Masonry were the major reasons for the Church's condemnation, we might envision some sort of rapprochement in the foreseeable future. [However,] The irreconcilable principles to which the 1983 letter refers remain the basic reason for the condemnation by the Catholic Church and other Christian bodies. We agree with the assessment of the German hierarchy, which studied the Masonic question between 1974 and 1980, and observed in part:

> Although it may be important to distinguish between favorable, neutral or hostile Masonry, with regard to the Church, the same distinction, in this context, leads to error because it insinuates that for Catholics, only membership in a hostile branch would be inadmissable.

If we try to make "plotting against the Church" the sole criterion for allowing or disallowing membership, we in effect are saying that we do not concern ourselves with the nature of an organization or what it teaches. By the same token, we should allow membership by Catholics in organizations of spiritualists, theosophists and occultists, so long as these groups do not plot against the Church. But the Church's historic stand has not been based primarily on whether the Masonic Lodges are hostile or neutral toward the Church, but on the principles for which the Lodge stands.

To grasp the fundamental objections to Freemasonry, we have to review briefly the history of the craft.

Unlike other craftsmen in the Middle Ages, the stonemasons who built the great cathedrals of Europe were forced to move from place to place to follow their occupation. To protect their skills and to recognize fellow masons, they devised a system of signs and passwords. These served the purpose of a union card. Their worksheds were called lodges.

With the decline of cathedral building, some of the lodges of stonemasons began to admit nonworking or honorary masons. In time the number of honorary free and accepted Masons outnumbered the working masons. They used the tools, symbols, signs, grips and passwords of the masons' trade union to create what we know as speculative Freemasonry. This new craft Masonry usually defines itself as "a peculiar system of morality, veiled in allegory and illustrated by symbols."

The Masons of early medieval times were Catholics, like

almost everyone else in Europe. But under the influence of deism, all traces of Christianity were excised from speculative Freemasonry. In the 1723 Book of Constitutions, the new attitude toward religious belief was spelled out: "A Mason is obliged by his tenure to obey the moral law; and if he rightly understands the art, he will never be a stupid atheist nor an irreligious libertine. But though in ancient times Masons were charged in every country to be of the religion of that country or nation, whatever it was, yet 'tis now thought more expedient only to oblige them to that religion in which all men agree, leaving their particular opinions to themselves."

Freemasonry as Universal Religion

Clearly, whatever constitutes "that religion in which all men agree," it is not Christianity or revealed religion. Masons, as Masons, believe in the fatherhood of God, the brotherhood of mankind and the immortality of the soul. These are beliefs which they maintain can be discovered by human reason. The inspiration of the Bible, the unique claims of Jesus Christ, the authority and teaching role of the Church, and the Sacraments as means of grace are "particular opinions" which Freemasons are asked to keep to themselves, rather than disturb the brothers in the Lodge.

A century ago, in his encyclical on Freemasonry, *Humanum Genus*, Leo XIII defined naturalism, which he saw as the primary objection to the Masonic system:

> Now the fundamental doctrine of the naturalists, which they sufficiently make known by their very name, is that human nature and human reason ought in all things be mistress and guide . . . For they deny that anything has been taught by God; they allow no dogma of religion or truth which cannot be understood by human intelligence nor any teacher who ought to be believed by reason of his authority.

In keeping with the naturalism of the Lodge, no prayers in the Blue lodges are ever offered in the name of Jesus Christ. God, whom Christians have been told to address as our Father, is worshipped as the deistic Great Architect of the Universe. As the authors of the recent article in the *Review of Religious Research* put it:

> The nature of the Masonic God is best seen in their favorite title for him: the Supreme Architect. The Masonic God is first of all a deistic God, who is found at the top of the ladder of Masonic wisdom. (Jolicoeur and Knowles, pp. 14-15).

In U.S. Freemasonry, all women, men under 21, and blacks are barred from Masonic initiation in regular lodges. Otherwise, only the atheist—technically the "stupid atheist"—and the "irreligious libertine" are unwelcome. By jettisoning the vestiges of Christianity, modern Freemasonry opened its doors to deists, Jews, Moslems, Hindus, Buddhists and any who acknowledge the existence of the Grand Architect of the Universe and who believe in the immortality of the soul. Perhaps a religious naturalism is better than no religious belief at all, but for the professing Christian it represents a retreat from the Gospel.

We can agree with Albert Pike when he wrote, "Every Masonic lodge is a temple of religion, and its teachings are instruction in religion." (*Morals and Dogma*, p. 213). Pike served as sovereign grand inspector of the Southern jurisdiction of the Scottish rite for many years and is sometimes considered American Freemasonry's most eminent philosopher. His book *Morals and Dogma* is traditionally presented to those who attain the 32nd degree of the Scottish rite.

Not only does Freemasonry see itself as *a* religion, but it sees itself as the *universal* religion, while Christianity is seen as simply another of the dozens of sects whose particular opinions have divided mankind over the ages. Again we may refer to Brother Pike:

But Masonry teaches, and has preserved in their purity, the cardinal tenets of the old primitive faith, which underlie and are the foundation of all religions. All that ever existed have had a basis of truth; all have overlaid that truth with error. (p. 161).

Religion, to obtain currency and influence with the great mass of mankind, must needs be alloyed with such an amount of error as to place it far below the standard attainable by the higher human capacities. (p. 224).

Catholicism was a vital truth in its earliest ages, but it became obsolete, and Protestantism arose, flourished, and deteriorated. (p. 38).

In his *Encyclopedia of Freemasonry*, Albert G. Mackey writes:

I contend without any sort of hesitation, that Masonry is, in every sense of the word, except one, and that its least philosophical, an eminently religious institution . . . that without this religious element, it would scarcely be worthy of cultivation by the wise and good . . . Who can deny that it is eminently a religious institution? . . . But the religion of Masonry is not sectarian . . . It is not Judaism, though there is nothing in it to offend a Jew; it is not Christianity, but there is nothing in it repugnant to the faith of a Christian. Its religion is that general one of nature and primitive revelation—handed down to us from some ancient and patriarchal priesthood—in which all men may agree and in which no men can differ. It inculcates the practice of virtue, but supplies no scheme of redemption for sin . . . Masonry, then, is indeed a religious institution; and on this ground mainly, if not alone, should the religious Mason defend it. (pp. 617-619).

Hannah comments: "On reading the ritual carefully, Masonry will be found to present itself as a complete and self-sufficient system of moral and spiritual guidance through this world and the next. It teaches one's whole duty to God and to man, and a way of justification by works which, if followed, will lead to salvation. Nowhere does it give the slightest hint that anything further is necessary to the religious life." (*Darkness Visible*, p. 40).

While religious, Freemasonry clearly rejects dogma and the possibility of absolute truth. After six years, the German [Catholic] episcopal conference reported its conclusion in the June 1980 issue of *Amtsblatt des Erbistums Koln*, pp. 102-111. On this particular point, the German hierarchy observed:

> The religious conception of the Mason is relativistic: All religions are competitive attempts to explain the truth about God which, in the last analysis, is unattainable. Therefore, only the language of Masonic symbols, which is ambiguous and left to the subjective interpretation of the individual Mason, is adapted to this truth about God.

Attitude toward Christ, The Bible

Some Protestant defenders of the Lodge try to deny its religious character. Other Protestants and Catholics ask, "What element is missing in Freemasonry which we find in a religion?" Freemasonry has a creed and ritual, prayers to the Great Architect of the Universe, an altar and temples, feast days, chaplains, an initiation ceremony, and a system of morality. As its funeral service makes plain, the Lodge promises its members salvation and entry into the Grand Lodge Above, if they follow the precepts of the craft.

The Lodge honors Jesus Christ as it honors Socrates, Buddha and Mohammed. It cannot acknowledge any special spiritual claims by Jesus, since this would violate the basis of Freemasonry.

True, other fraternal and service organizations appoint chaplains and include prayers in their meetings, but the claims to a superior path to spiritual advancement and a superior morality are peculiar to Freemasonry.

Every Lodge works with an open Bible on its altar, and

to some Masons this seems to affirm its Christian orientation. The preferred term and the one used in English Free-masonry is the Volume of the Sacred Law. That no special authority is attached to the Old and New Testaments is clear since a lodge of Moslems may substitute the Koran, a predominantly Hindu lodge, the Vedas, etc. As the Digest of Masonic Law makes clear,

> To say that a candidate professes a belief in the divine authority of the Bible is a serious innovation in the very body of Masonry. The Jews, the Chinese, the Turks, each reject either the Old or the New Testament, or both, and yet we see no good reason why they should not be made Masons. In fact, Blue Lodge Masonry has nothing what-ever to do with the Bible. It is not founded on the Bible. If it were, it would not be Masonry. (p. 206).

Again we turn to Brother Pike:

> The Bible is an indispensable part of the furniture of a Christian lodge, only because it is the sacred book of the Christian religion. The Hebrew Pentateuch in a Hebrew lodge and the Koran in a Mohammedan one belong on the altar; and one of these, and the square and the compass, properly understood are the Great Lights by which a Mason must walk and work. The obligation of the candidate is always to be taken on the sacred book or books of his religion, that he may deem it more solemn and binding; and therefore it was that you were asked of what religion you were. We have no other concern with your religious creed. (p. 11).

Use of Oaths

The second major reason for the Church's hostility [to Masonry] is the Masonic oath, or rather, the series of oaths required of initiates. Unlike some of the Protestant sects, such as the Mennonites or Quakers, the Roman Catholic Church has interpreted the biblical injunction against swearing to allow for exceptions in serious cases, e.g., in a court of law.

The use of solemn oaths taken on the Bible in order to join a fraternal society or advance to its higher degrees has never been countenanced [by the Catholic Church]. Objectively speaking, those who swear such oaths are guilty of either vain or rash swearing. For most American Masons, the oaths are given for what turns out to be the supposed secrecy of a few passwords and handshakes. Anyone who has investigated Masonry knows what these "secrets" are anyway. In fact, someone has said that the greatest secret about Freemasonry is that there are no secrets. If there are not, then Christians have no justification for making such solemn oaths. Hannah posed the basic dilemma of the Masonic oaths when he wrote:

> Either the oaths mean what they say or they do not. If they do mean what they say, then the candidate is entering into a pact consenting to his own murder by barbarous torture and mutilation should he break it. If they do not mean what they say, then he is swearing highsounding schoolboy nonsense on the Bible, which verges on blasphemy. (*Darkness Visible*, p. 21).

For example, this is the oath of the master Mason's degree (each grand lodge controls its own ritual, so there may be minor variations in wording from state to state):

> I, (name), of my own free will and accord, in the presence of Almighty God, and his worshipful lodge, erected to him and dedicated to the holy Sts. John, do hereby and hereon most solemnly and sincerely promise and swear that I will always hail, ever conceal and never reveal any of the secrets, arts, parts, point or points of the master Masons' degree to any person or persons whomsoever, except that it be to a true and lawful brother of this degree, or in a regularly constituted lodge of master Masons, nor unto him or them, until by strict trial, due examination

or lawful information, I shall have found him or them as lawfully entitled to the same as I am myself.

I furthermore promise and swear that I will stand to and abide by all laws, rules and regulations of the master Mason's degree and of the lodge of which I may hereafter become a member, as far as the same shall come to my knowledge; and that I will ever maintain and support the constitution, laws and edicts of the grand lodge under which the same shall be holden.

Further, that I will acknowledge and obey all due signs and summonses sent to me from a master Masons' lodge or given me by a brother of that degree, if within the length of my cable tow.

Further, that I will always aid and assist all poor, distressed, worthy master Masons, their widows and orphans, knowing them to be such, as far as their necessities may require and my ability permit, without material injury to myself and family.

Further, that I will keep a worthy brother master Mason's secrets inviolable when communicated to and received by me as such, murder and treason excepted.

Further, that I will not aid nor be present at the initiation, passing or raising of a woman, an old man in his dotage, a young man in his nonage, an atheist, a madman or a fool, knowing them to be such.

Further, that I will not sit in a lodge of clandestine-made Masons nor converse on the subject of Masonry with a clandestine-made Mason nor one who has been expelled or suspended from a lodge, while under that sentence, knowing him or them to be such.

Further, I will not cheat, wrong nor defraud a master Mason's lodge nor a brother of this degree knowingly, nor supplant him in any of his laudable undertakings, but will give him due and timely notice, that he may ward off all danger.

Further, that I will not knowingly strike a brother master Mason or otherwise do him personal violence in anger, except in the necessary defense of my family or property.

Further, that I will not have illegal carnal intercourse with a master Mason's wife, his mother, sister or daughter, knowing them to be such, nor suffer the same to be done by others, if in my power to prevent.

Further, that I will not give the grand Masonic word, in any other manner or form than that in which I shall receive it and then in a low breath.

Further, that I will not give the grand hailing sign of distress except in case of the most imminent danger, in a just and lawful lodge, or for the benefit of instruction; and if ever I should see it given or hear the words accompanying it by a worthy brother in distress, I will fly to his relief, if there is a greater probability of saving his life than losing my own.

All this I most solemnly, sincerely promise and swear, with a firm and steady resolution to perform the same, without any hesitation, mental reservation or secret evasion of mind whatever, binding myself under no less penalty than that of having my body severed in two, my bowels taken from thence and burned to ashes, the ashes scattered before the four winds of heaven, that no more remembrance might be had of so vile and wicked a wretch as I would be, should I ever knowingly violate this my master Mason's obligation. So help me God, and keep me steadfast in the due performance of the same.

Opposition of Christian Churches Other than Catholic

Like opposition to abortion, opposition to Freemasonry is often seen as solely a Roman Catholic position. But the Catholic Church is hardly the only Christian body to recognize the essential difference between the Masonic and Christian religions. In fact, most Christians around the world belong to churches which forbid or discourage Masonic affiliation.

The Inter-Orthodox commission which met on Mount Athos (1933) and represented all the autocephalous Eastern Orthodox churches characterized Freemasonry as a "false and anti-Christian system." This remains the position of Orthodoxy.

Other groups hostile to Lodge membership include many branches of Lutheranism, the Christian Reformed Church, most Pentecostals, the Church of the Nazarene, the Seventh-day Adventists, the Holiness churches, the Quakers, the United Brethren in Christ, the Mennonites, the Free Methodists, the Church of the Brethren, the Assemblies of God, the Wesleyans, the Regular Baptists, the Salvation Army and significant minorities in such mainline churches as the Episcopal.

Jehovah's Witnesses and the Church of Jesus Christ of Latter-day Saints also oppose Masonry. Joseph Smith, Jr. joined the Masonic Lodge in Nauvoo, Illinois, and turned to the Lodge ritual to find elements for his secret temple rites. Masons in the mob which stormed the Carthage jail and murdered the prophet ignored his grand hailing sign of distress. The Grand Lodge of Utah refuses to initiate a Mormon, and any Mormon who joins the Lodge outside of Utah finds his advancement in the hierarchy severely curtailed.

Obviously the problem all these religious groups have with Freemasonry is not its anti-Catholic character.

The Lutheran Cyclopedia explains: "While frankly anti-Christian in its French, German and Italian branches, Freemasonry in England and the United States has always called itself a supporter of the morality and doctrine of the Protestant church. Very few candidates realize that they are joining an organization which is essentially antagonistic to the Christian belief in the inspiration of the Bible and the divinity of Jesus Christ." (p. 392).

For millions of other American Protestants, such as Baptists, Methodists, Presbyterians and Episcopalians, dual membership in the church and the Lodge is acceptable. Individual members, however, may have reservations about the compatibility of the Grand Architect of the Universe and the triune God. British Methodism has been less favorably inclined toward Freemasonry, perhaps reflecting John Wesley's observation about the Lodge: "What an amazing banter on all mankind is Freemasonry." Currently a commission of English Methodists is studying the Lodge question. Within the past year a general synod of the Church of England also voted to investigate Freemasonry to determine if Masonic beliefs and practices are compatible with Christianity.

Since neither the religious naturalism nor the required oaths of Freemasonry are ever likely to change, the hope that these irreconcilable principles can ever be reconciled is dim. Another objection to U.S. Masonry which should give pause to any Christian is the blatant racism of the Lodges. This may someday change, but the Lodges have lagged far behind the rest of American society in this matter.

Simply stated, the predominant Blue Lodges refuse to initiate anyone known to be black. There is a single exception: Alpha Lodge No. 116 of Newark, New Jersey, which is recognized by the Grand Lodge of New Jersey. Stories have circulated in recent years about a black candidate in Wisconsin or some other state being initiated, but these are unverified.

Blacks long ago established their own parallel organization of Masonry known as Prince Hall, along with Black counterparts of the Scottish rite, Shrine, etc. These are viewed as clandestine and irregular by white Masonry. A Prince Hall Mason cannot be admitted to a meeting of the Blue Lodges, and a Black man who evidences an interest in Masonry will be politely directed to a Prince Hall lodge.

This situation is an embarrassment to many American Masons, as well as to the Grand Lodge of England, the mother Lodge, which does not practice such racial discrimination. Sooner or later, we believe, the American Lodges will have to re-examine their racist standards and bring them into alignment with the rest of society.

Ecumenical Attitudes

No doubt the ecumenical spirit has contributed to the desire on the part of many that the Church relax its ban on Masonic membership. Maintenance of the ban may indeed hamper some ecumenical efforts, but a few things should be kept in mind. As we saw, most of the world's Christians now belong to churches which forbid or discourage Masonic membership. This may be a situation in which those who belong to denominations which allow membership should ask themselves why Roman Catholics, Eastern Orthodox, many Lutherans and fellow Protestants take the stand they do against the Lodge. Fr. Walton Hannah observed, "No church that has seriously investigated the religious teachings and implications of Freemasonry has ever yet failed to condemn it." (*Darkness Visible*, p. 78).

In his critique of Freemasonry, the distinguished Anglican theologian, Dr. Hubert S. Box, examined the claim of the Lodge that its chief purpose is to teach men about the nature of God and observed:

> But to teach men about the nature of God is properly the responsibility of the church, by virtue of its divine commission, so that the church, being aware that some of its members are receiving instructions on the nature of God within the barricaded secrecy of a rival teaching body having no divine commission to exercise such a function, has the right to make inquiries as to the sort of instruction they are receiving. (*The Nature of Freemasonry*, p. 5).

The Catholic Church an other churches need not apologize for their stand on Lodge membership. One of the boasts of Freemasonry has been that it fosters brotherhood; the Church's refusal to allow dual membership in the Church and the Lodge may seem mean-spirited to some. We can, however, ask our non-Catholic friends which institution best exemplifies brotherhood: American Freemasonry or the Church, which is open to men and women, blacks and whites, young and old, rich and poor?

Does this mean that antagonism between Freemasonry and the Christian churches which forbid membership should be fostered? In no way. Dialogue between Christians and Masons can lessen hostility between these groups. Co-operation in civic and charitable works can be encouraged.[2]

---

2. Since Pope Leo XIII stated that "to join with these men [Freemasons] or in any way to help them cannot be lawful" (see pp. 5-6), it would seem that "co-operation" between Catholics and Freemasons would be appropriate and moral only under the strictest of conditions, and that it would be far preferable

Some Catholics believe the most fantastic things about
Masonry and should be helped to form a rational judgment
on the Lodge. Some Masons see the Church of Rome as the
Church of the Inquisition, the Crusaders, the prop for dis-
credited monarchies. No one benefits from such caricatures.

The Catholic Church now engages in dialogue with many
Protestant, Eastern Orthodox and even non-Christian bodies.
The fact that a Roman Catholic may not at the same time
profess Islam does not mean that fruitful Catholic-Moslem
dialogue is impossible or useless.

Problem of Catholics as Recent Members

The serious problem of Catholic men who joined a
Masonic Lodge during those recent years in which such
membership was apparently tolerated remains, and the
approach to this problem requires great tact. There are
32nd-degree Masons who are daily communicants and active
members of Catholic parishes.

In good faith many of these men had asked their pastors
and/or bishops for permission to join the Lodge. Some converts were received into the Church during these years and
were not asked to relinquish their Masonic affiliation. (In
Freemasonry, no one is supposed to be solicited to join the
Lodge, and no one is supposed to become a Mason by the
consent of another. Some Masons viewed the 1974 statement
by Cardinal Seper as requiring Catholics to obtain the consent of the bishop in order to petition for membership, and
as such this constituted unMasonic conduct.)

One possible solution for these men would be to allow
them to retain passive membership in their Masonic Lodges.
The apostolic delegation was empowered to approve such

for Catholics to perform "civic and charitable works" with other Catholics, rather
than with persons who deny, or at least put no importance on, many or all of the
teachings of Christ. It has been the author's experience that Catholics sometimes
end up getting involved in Freemasonry precisely because of too close a co-
operation with Masons in various activities. Similar cautions would apply regarding
"dialogue" between the Church and Freemasonry. —*Bro. C. M.*

passive membership in a decree of the Holy Office of May 31, 1911, in *Una Scrantonen*, if the following conditions were verified:

1. If petitioners gave their names to the sect in good faith before they knew it was condemned.

2. If there is no scandal or if it can be removed with an appropriate declaration, they can remain in the sect passively and for a time, so they do not lose the right to benefits, abstaining from communion with the group and from any participation, even material.

3. If serious harm would result for them or their family from their renunciation.

4. If there is no danger of perversion for them or their family, especially in the case of sickness or death.

This possible solution is far from perfect. In effect the Church is saying that, if an individual meets these conditions, he may pay his dues but not attend meetings, read Masonic literature, consent to a Masonic funeral, etc.[3] In other words, "You may remain a Mason, but don't take Masonry seriously."

(Many bishops and priests seem to think that the Masonic Lodge is a fraternal benefit society similar to the Knights of Columbus. Masons may expect some measure of financial assistance from fellow Masons, as may their widows and orphans, but Freemasonry is not an insurance company. Masons do not buy insurance from their grand lodges, and resignation from the Lodge does not mean forfeiture of insurance benefits.)

In some respects, most Masons are passive members. The week-to-week business of a Masonic Lodge is simply dull and consists mainly in putting candidates through the three degrees. A Lodge with hundreds of members may have difficulty rounding up enough members to conduct the ritual. American Masons who read much more than an occasional

---

3. No. 2 above stipulates that an individual would be permitted to retain passive membership *"for a time"* (and only under the required conditions).—*Bro. C. M.*

Masonic newsletter are rare, and most are unaware of the standard Masonic books by Pike, Mackey, et al. They may absorb the naturalism of Freemasonry unconsciously but seldom make a serious study of its Weltanschauung [philosophy of life]. Not to be smug about it, we should acknowledge that millions of Catholics are also passive or nominal members of the Church.

Except in certain communities, often in the South or rural areas, the Masonic Lodge has lost most of its erstwhile attraction. The term often applied to English Freemasonry, the "Mafia of the Mediocre," seems evermore applicable to the American Lodges. A recent article in the *Texas Monthly* (December 1983) points up the problems for the Lodge in a state which has traditionally had a strong grand lodge.

> Unless enrollment trends change soon, by the turn of the century, few Masons will be left in Texas. The number of people who ask to join has been declining in both orders (white and black lodges) since the years immediately following World War II. . . . Other fraternal orders that have fared better, such as the Lions and Rotary clubs, are wired to commerce; they are practical clubs for modern men, and joining the Masons (by application), with all their traditions and odd rituals of brotherhood, is akin to joining a college fraternity, but today's men of the world no longer seem interested in whiling away their hours by fraternizing in the lodge or memorizing ritual codes.

The Lodges have conspicuously failed to attract the diploma elite. Even politicians no longer see the need to wear the Masonic apron. Eisenhower, Kennedy, Nixon, Carter and Reagan managed to win the White House without Masonic affiliation. Johnson received the first or entered-apprentice degree, but never advanced to master Mason.

This suggests that the requests from Catholic men to join the Lodge are not likely to increase. The opportunities for making business contacts and enjoying fellowship in other organizations are so plentiful that no Catholic need feel he is sacrificing much by following the precepts of his Church in shunning the Lodge. He can join the Kiwanis, Lions, Elks, Eagles, Chamber of Commerce, Jaycees, Moose, Knights of Columbus, American Legion, VFW, Serra Club, Optimists, Exchange, Rotary and dozens of other civic and service organizations.

A separate pastoral problem arises when we turn to the affiliated Masonic organizations, which enroll both Masons and non-Masons. An example would be the Order of the Eastern Star, whose membership is open to master Masons and their wives, widows, mothers, sisters, and daughters. Thousands of Catholic women fall into this category. Other Masonic-related groups include the DeMolay order for young men, Job's Daughters and Rainbow Girls for young women, and the Acacia college fraternity.

Although the possibility of scandal may exist, the fact remains that these women and young people do not swear Masonic oaths and are not considered Masons. We can apply the general canonical principle that "favorable laws are to be interpreted broadly and odious laws are to be interpreted strictly" (*Odios a restringenda, favorabilia extendenda*). This would not mean that pastors would encourage such affiliation.

The Catholic Church should not launch any kind of new vendetta[4] against Freemasonry and should welcome the lessening of anti-Catholicism, whether in the Lodge, the Southern Baptist Convention, the Lutheran Church (Missouri Synod) or any other group. At the same time, it must affirm that membership by Catholics in the Lodge is inappropriate.[5]

---

4. Professor Whalen's phrase "new vendetta" gives the impression that the Church acted in a vindictive way against Freemasonry in the past. I do not believe that to be the case! For sure, an educational campaign directed toward Catholics who are Freemasons should be undertaken by the Church. The official documents in these appendices are a positive initial step.—*Bro. C. M.*

5. Moreover, Catholic membership in Freemasonry is actually forbidden by the Church. See the 1983 Declaration, Appendix B above.—*Bro. C. M.*

Conclusion

My conclusion is the same as that of the German episcopal conference: "In-depth research on the ritual and on the Masonic mentality makes it clear that it is impossible to belong to the Catholic Church and to Freemasonry at the same time."

The false ecumenism which seeks to ignore basic differences between Masonic naturalism and Christianity, and the desire of a few Catholic men to find in the Lodge a fellowship, a better chance for promotion or a wider base of customers than they can find through other organizations are no reason to ignore the serious objections to Freemasonry raised by the Church.

Perhaps some accommodations may be made for pastoral reasons in exceptional cases. Converts might be permitted to retain passive membership. Those Catholic men who joined the Lodge in good faith during the recent years of confusion might be offered the same option.[6] Membership in Masonic-related organizations such as the Eastern Star should be discouraged, but does not carry the same penalty of exclusion from the Eucharist. Otherwise, the position of the Church remains what it has been for many years: Catholics in the United States and elsewhere may not be Freemasons.

(Used with permission of U.S. Bishops' Committe for Pastoral Research and Practices. This report and the foregoing Statement are the texts as published in Origins, *official publication of the USCC, June 27, 1985, pp. 83-92.)*

---

6. We note that Professor Whalen presents the "passive membership for a time" solution only as a possible solution for these "exceptional cases." (See the list of strict conditions on page 61.) The *norm* for a Catholic Freemason, of course, would be to resign officially and to sever all ties with Freemasonry. See Appendix E: Questions and Answers.—*Bro. C. M.*

Appendix E

Questions and Answers

1. May Catholics join the Freemasons?
No. To do so would be a grave sin, excluding one from receiving Holy Communion. (See p. 35).

2. Why is it so wrong to join the Freemasons?
Simply put, Freemasonry is an anti-Christian religion which openly disavows basic Christian truths, such as, for example, the divinity of Jesus Christ. No conscientious Catholic, or Protestant Christian can subscribe to its beliefs. (See pp. 17-20).

3. But I know Catholics in Masonry who were told by their pastor it was OK to join! Why is this?
In recent decades a great deal of confusion arose when wrong information was disseminated, even in the Catholic media, that membership in the Freemasons was permitted under some circumstances. This simply was not true. (See pp. 41-43).

4. What is the latest statement from Rome regarding Catholics being Freemasons?
On November 26, 1983, the Sacred Congregation for the Doctrine of the Faith issued a Declaration on Masonic Associations which stated: "The negative posi-

tion of the Church in regard to Masonic associations remains unchanged, since their basic principles have always been considered irreconcilable with the teachings of the Church, and consequently membership in them remains forbidden. The faithful who belong to Masonic associations are in a state of grave sin and may not receive Holy Communion." (See pp. 35-36).

5. **What should such Catholics in Freemasonry do to correct their situation?**

First, *and at the very least*, they should become *passive* members by no longer attending Lodge meetings or other Masonic activities. Second, they should see their parish priest concerning other requirements (see pp. 60-61, 63-64 for guidance), seeking of course absolution in the Sacrament of Penance. Third, they should send a letter of demit (formal resignation) to their local Lodge. This formal letter of demit may not be *required* by the Church, but it certainly helps to make the break with Freemasonry complete. A sentence or two stating the renunciation of Freemasonry as incompatible with one's Catholic Faith is sufficient.

6. **What is the attitude of Protestant churches toward Freemasonry?**

Though many Protestants are in Freemasonry, more and more Protestant denominations are declaring Freemasonry incompatible with Christianity. (See pp. 56-58).

7. **Some of my Protestant relatives are into Freemasonry but would never accept Catholic literature on the subject. Whom can I refer them to?**

One resource is the H. R. Taylor Ministries, Box 12, Newtonville, NY 12128. This ministry was established by a Protestant minister who converted from Freemasonry. A wide variety of literature is available from them, including statements issued by many of the Protestant denominations' official church bodies. Incidentally, Taylor Ministries strongly recommends that a Christian leaving Freemasonry send a letter of demit to the local Lodge. This is done as a means of evangelization, since a letter of demit must be read to the members of the Lodge.

Appendix F

Kadosh—30th Degree

The following material is taken from the *Scottish Rite Ritual*, Vol. II, 1892 edition, Ezra Cook, publisher, Chicago, IL; now Lauterer Corp. The actions portrayed here are confirmed by more recent Masonic works such as the 1970 combined edition, Vol. I, p. 433, of *A New Encyclopaedia of Freemasonry*, edited by Arthur Edward Waite. According to *The Freemason's Pocket Reference Book*, 1983 edition, p. 180, the 30th Degree Knight Kadosh is always fully worked under every Supreme Council.

In the *Scottish Rite Ritual*, Vol. II (p. 257), the candidate for Knight Kadosh is brought before a platform on which there rest three skulls; ". . . the one on the left is surmounted by a Pope's triple crown. . . ." Immediately after taking the first of the four oaths of the degree (p. 260), the candidate, following the example and instruction of the Thrice Puissant Grand Master, stabs the skull crowned with the Pope's crown and says, "Down with imposture, down with crime." It is important to realize that in this degree the word "imposture" always refers to the Pope's role as Vicar of Christ.

A similar ceremony with different wording is also performed on a skull wearing a king's crown. Shortly thereafter the candidate is warned (p. 261) that should he ever betray his oath, he would be subject to punishment, even death. As the ritual of initiation continues, during the third of the four oaths, the candidate binds himself under penalty of death. (pp. 269-270).

A funeral urn is now placed on a mausoleum, to the right of which ". . . is a regal crown; on the left a popish tiara." (p. 271). Elsewhere is an altar containing a human skull inlaid with silver, a decanter of red wine, and a loaf of white bread. Later (pp. 284-285), after a fourth oath is taken, during which "imposture" is denounced, those present drink wine from the silver-inlaid skull and eat the bread.

Afterward (p. 286), the candidate is instructed by the Thrice Puissant Grand Master concerning the papal tiara: "This represents the Tiara of the cruel and cowardly Pontiff, who sacrificed to his ambition the illustrious order of those Knights Templar of whom we are the true successors. A crown of gold and precious stones ill befits the humble head of one who pretends to be successor, the Vicar, of Jesus of Nazareth. It is therefore the crown of an imposter, and it is in the name of him who said, 'neither be ye called Masters,' that we trample it under our feet." Following this instruction the papal tiara is thrown to the floor, and all present trample it underfoot while shouting, "Down with imposture!"

The candidate, having thus ". . . discarded all stupid and vulgar prejudices," is then knighted Kadosh by the Grand Master.

Appendix G

Sources

1. Pope Leo XIII. *Humanum Genus*, encyclical letter on Freemasonry, April 20, 1884. Reprinted by TAN Books and Publishers, Inc., 1978.

2. Pike, Albert. *Morals and Dogma.* Richmond, VA: L.H. Jenkins, Inc. Edition Book Manufacturers, 1871; March, 1947. Official collection and source book of Freemasonry's governing principles used by Freemasons in the U.S. and Canada for the past century. It was prepared in 1871 for the Supreme Council of the Thirty-third Degree of the Scottish Rite Freemasons for the Southern Jurisdiction of the U.S. by its Supreme Commander, Albert Pike. The book is a series of "lectures" designed to explain Degrees one through thirty-two. Copies usually are given only to those who have been accepted into the thirty-second Degree. Recipients are required never to allow the book to leave their possession, and to make provision for its return to the Scottish Rite upon their deaths. Copies of this secret work do occasionally fall into the hands of Church authorities and other non-Masons, due to defections from the Masons and to inevitable human lapses. Marytown's copy came from the estate of a priest who had received one of these.

3. Fisher, Paul A. *Behind the Lodge Door: Church, State and Freemasonry in America.* Bowie, MD: Shield Publishing,

Inc., 1988. Reprinted by TAN Books and Publishers, Inc., Rockford, IL, 1991 and 1994.

4. Hannah, Walton. *Darkness Visible: A Revelation and Interpretation of Freemasonry*. Chulmleigh, Devon, England: Britons (Augustine) Publishing Co., 1975.

5. Shaw, Jim and McKenney, Tom. *The Deadly Deception*. Lafayette, LA: Huntington House, Inc., 1988. This book is an autobiographical account of the experiences of Jim Shaw during his years in Freemasonry. Now a Protestant minister, Rev. Shaw had achieved the 33rd Degree before his conversion to Christianity.

6. McClenachan, Charles T. *The Book of the Ancient and Accepted Scottish Rite*. McClenachan, a 33rd-Degree Mason, was a past Grand Master of Ceremonies of the Supreme Council, Northern Jurisdiction, U.S. (The book is equivilant to *Morals and Dogma* described in no. 2 above.)

7. *The Rites of the Catholic Church*. New York, NY: Pueblo Publishing Co., 1976.

8. Epperson, A. Ralph. *The New World Order*. Tuscon, AZ: Publius Press, 1990.

9. Freemantle, Brian. *The Octopus*. London, England: Orion Books, Ltd., 1995.

Recommended Reading

Humanum Genus; *Behind the Lodge Door*; *The Deadly Deception*; and *The New World Order*.

If you have enjoyed this book, consider making your next selection from among the following . . .

Prices subject to change.

Seven Capital Sins. *Benedictine Sisters* 3.00
Confession—Its Fruitful Practice. *Ben. Srs.* 3.00
Sermons of the Curé of Ars. *Vianney* 15.00
St. Antony of the Desert. *St. Athanasius* 7.00
Is It a Saint's Name? *Fr. William Dunne* 3.00
St. Pius V—His Life, Times, Miracles. *Anderson* 7.00
Who Is Therese Neumann? *Fr. Charles Carty.* 3.50
Martyrs of the Coliseum. *Fr. O'Reilly.* 21.00
Way of the Cross. *St. Alphonsus Liguori.* 1.50
Way of the Cross. *Franciscan version.* 1.50
How Christ Said the First Mass. *Fr. Meagher* 21.00
Too Busy for God? Think Again! *D'Angelo* 7.00
St. Bernadette Soubirous. *Trochu* 21.00
Pope Pius VII. *Anderson* 16.50
Treatise on the Love of God. 1 Vol. *de Sales. Mackey, Trans.* 27.50
Confession Quizzes. *Radio Replies Press* 2.50
St. Philip Neri. *Fr. V. J. Matthews.* 7.50
St. Louise de Marillac. *Sr. Vincent Regnault* 7.50
The Old World and America. *Rev. Philip Furlong.* 21.00
Prophecy for Today. *Edward Connor* 7.50
The Book of Infinite Love. *Mother de la Touche* 7.50
Chats with Converts. *Fr. M. D. Forrest.* 13.50
The Church Teaches. *Church Documents* 18.00
Conversation with Christ. *Peter T. Rohrbach* 12.50
Purgatory and Heaven. *J. P. Arendzen.* 6.00
Liberalism Is a Sin. *Sarda y Salvany* 9.00
Spiritual Legacy of Sr. Mary of the Trinity. *van den Broek* 13.00
The Creator and the Creature. *Fr. Frederick Faber* 17.50
Radio Replies. 3 Vols. *Frs. Rumble and Carty* 48.00
Convert's Catechism of Catholic Doctrine. *Fr. Geiermann* 5.00
Incarnation, Birth, Infancy of Jesus Christ. *St. Alphonsus* 13.50
Light and Peace. *Fr. R. P. Quadrupani* 8.00
Dogmatic Canons & Decrees of Trent, Vat. I. *Documents* 11.00
The Evolution Hoax Exposed. *A. N. Field* 9.00
The Primitive Church. *Fr. D. I. Lanslots.* 12.50
The Priest, the Man of God. *St. Joseph Cafasso* 16.00
Blessed Sacrament. *Fr. Frederick Faber* 20.00
Christ Denied. *Fr. Paul Wickens* 3.50
New Regulations on Indulgences. *Fr. Winfrid Herbst* 3.00
A Tour of the Summa. *Msgr. Paul Glenn* 22.50
Latin Grammar. *Scanlon and Scanlon* 18.00
A Brief Life of Christ. *Fr. Rumble* 3.50
Marriage Quizzes. *Radio Replies Press* 2.50
True Church Quizzes. *Radio Replies Press.* 2.50
The Secret of the Rosary. *St. Louis De Montfort.* 5.00
Mary, Mother of the Church. *Church Documents* 5.00
The Sacred Heart and the Priesthood. *de la Touche* 10.00
Revelations of St. Bridget. *St. Bridget of Sweden* 4.50
Magnificent Prayers. *St. Bridget of Sweden* 2.00
The Happiness of Heaven. *Fr. J. Boudreau* 10.00
St. Catherine Labouré of the Miraculous Medal. *Dirvin* 16.50
The Glories of Mary. *St. Alphonsus Liguori* 21.00
Three Conversions/Spiritual Life. *Garrigou-Lagrange, O.P.* 7.00

Prices subject to change.

Prices subject to change.

St. Margaret Clitherow—"The Pearl of York." *Monro* 6.00
St. Vincent Ferrer. *Fr. Pradel, O.P.* 9.00
The Life of Father De Smet. *Fr. Laveille, S.J.* 18.00
Glories of Divine Grace. *Fr. Matthias Scheeben* 18.00
Holy Eucharist—Our All. *Fr. Lukas Etlin* 3.00
Hail Holy Queen (from *Glories of Mary*). *St. Alphonsus* 9.00
Novena of Holy Communions. *Lovasik* 2.50
Brief Catechism for Adults. *Cogan* 12.50
The Cath. Religion—Illus./Expl. for Child, Adult, Convert. *Burbach* 12.50
Eucharistic Miracles. *Joan Carroll Cruz* 16.50
The Incorruptibles. *Joan Carroll Cruz* 16.50
Secular Saints: 250 Lay Men, Women & Children. PB. *Cruz.* 35.00
Pope St. Pius X. *F. A. Forbes* 11.00
St. Alphonsus Liguori. *Frs. Miller and Aubin* 18.00
Self-Abandonment to Divine Providence. *Fr. de Caussade, S.J.* 22.50
The Song of Songs—A Mystical Exposition. *Fr. Arintero, O.P.* 21.50
Prophecy for Today. *Edward Connor* 7.50
Saint Michael and the Angels. *Approved Sources* 9.00
Dolorous Passion of Our Lord. *Anne C. Emmerich* 18.00
Modern Saints—Their Lives & Faces, Book I. *Ann Ball.* 21.00
Modern Saints—Their Lives & Faces, Book II. *Ann Ball* 23.00
Our Lady of Fatima's Peace Plan from Heaven. *Booklet* 1.00
Divine Favors Granted to St. Joseph. *Père Binet* 7.50
St. Joseph Cafasso—Priest of the Gallows. *St. John Bosco* 6.00
Catechism of the Council of Trent. *McHugh/Callan* 27.50
The Foot of the Cross. *Fr. Faber.* 18.00
The Rosary in Action. *John Johnson* 12.00
Padre Pio—The Stigmatist. *Fr. Charles Carty* 16.50
Why Squander Illness? *Frs. Rumble & Carty* 4.00
Fatima—The Great Sign. *Francis Johnston* 12.00
Heliotropium—Conformity of Human Will to Divine. *Drexelius* 15.00
Charity for the Suffering Souls. *Fr. John Nageleisen* 18.00
Devotion to the Sacred Heart of Jesus. *Verheylezoon* 16.50
Who Is Padre Pio? *Radio Replies Press* 3.00
The Stigmata and Modern Science. *Fr. Charles Carty* 2.50
St. Anthony—The Wonder Worker of Padua. *Stoddard* 7.00
The Precious Blood. *Fr. Faber* 16.50
The Holy Shroud & Four Visions. *Fr. O'Connell* 3.50
Clean Love in Courtship. *Fr. Lawrence Lovasik* 4.50
The Secret of the Rosary. *St. Louis De Montfort* 5.00
The History of Antichrist. *Rev. P. Huchede* 4.00
Where We Got the Bible. *Fr. Henry Graham* 8.00
Hidden Treasure—Holy Mass. *St. Leonard* 7.50
Imitation of the Sacred Heart of Jesus. *Fr. Arnoudt.* 18.50
The Life & Glories of St. Joseph. *Edward Thompson* 16.50
Père Lamy. *Biver.* 15.00
Humility of Heart. *Fr. Cajetan da Bergamo* 9.00
The Curé D'Ars. *Abbé Francis Trochu* 24.00
Love, Peace and Joy. (St. Gertrude). *Prévot* 8.00

At your Bookdealer or direct from the Publisher.
Toll-Free 1-800-437-5876   *Fax 815-226-7770*
Tel. 815-226-7777   ***www.tanbooks.com***

Prices subject to change.

FREEMASONRY

MANKIND'S HIDDEN ENEMY

FREEMASONRY: MANKIND'S HIDDEN ENEMY is a short, incisive examinat
of the nature of Freemasonry, written to give the busy reader a brief, cl
overview of the subject and to convince Catholics of our time that
Church still forbids them to join this cult—and to give the reasons w
Quoting Pope Leo XIII's famous encyclical *Humanum Genus* (1884)—whicl
still the Church's classic condemnation of Freemasonry—the author proves t
Freemasonry is a secret society, one that even its own members do not know
exact objectives of, and whose members swear blind obedience to their lead
even under pain of death. He shows that Freemasonry is a religion of naturali
and aims at promoting naturalism and human reason over the influence of
Church upon society, especially in the secularizing of marriage and educati
Though portraying itself as a friend and benefactor of all mankind, Freemaso
actually denigrates God, Jesus Christ, monotheism and religion, and works to n
lify the effects of all religion—but especially the Catholic religion—upon soci
and individuals. It accomplishes this end by fostering indifference to religion :
the idea that one religion is as good as another, but also through immorality, wh
destroys a person's idealism and respect for truth.

Very importantly, the author discusses the Catholic confusion ab
Freemasonry dating from the 1970's, showing that the Church has not changed .
traditional stance against the cult. The book includes the latest declaration fr
Rome regarding Freemasonry, and tells Catholics in Freemasonry what they sho
do to rectify their situation. It also discusses the remarkable similarities betwe
Freemasonry and the New Age Movement, how Masonry is linked to anci
paganism and to the mafia, and how it has in the past cooperated with Sociali
and Communism. Bro. Charles includes a little-known statement from
Maximilian Kolbe regarding Freemasonry's main strategy against Catholic
plus St. Maximilian's inspired counter-strategy. A series of brief, enligh
Appendices rounds out the picture this book draws of Freemasonry—wl
clearly portrays as evil—so that in the end, one has an excellent understand
exactly what is wrong with Freemasonry and just why a Catholic may not jc

*"Let no man think that he may for any reason whatso-
ever join the Masonic sect, if he values his Catholic name
and his eternal salvation . . ."* —Pope Leo XIII
Humanum Genus

TAN

Out of My Mind

Late Night Contemplations About Trauma and Neglect

By Ruth Cohn, MFT